Maugham

SPLENDID ISOLATION

Splendid Isolation

A study of ideas concerning Britain's international position and foreign policy during the later years of the third Marquis of Salisbury

Christopher Howard

READER IN HISTORY,
UNIVERSITY OF LONDON, KING'S COLLEGE

Macmillan
LONDON · MELBOURNE · TORONTO
St Martin's Press
NEW YORK
1967

MACMILLAN AND COMPANY LIMITED
Little Essex Street London WC2
also Bombay Madras Calcutta Melbourne
THE MACMILLAN COMPANY OF CANADA LIMITED
70 Bond Street Toronto 2
ST MARTIN'S PRESS
175 Fifth Avenue New York NY 10010

Library of Congress catalog card no. 67–19736

PRINTED IN GREAT BRITAIN BY
ROBERT MACLEHOSE & CO. LTD
THE UNIVERSITY PRESS, GLASGOW

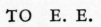

TO E. E.

Contents

ACKNOWLEDGMENTS

I WISH to acknowledge the gracious permission of Her Majesty the Queen to make use of material in the Royal Archives at Windsor Castle.

I should also like to express my thanks for many kindnesses to the Queen's Librarian, Mr Robert Mackworth-Young; to the Registrar of the Royal Archives, Miss J. Langton; to her predecessor, Miss E. Price-Hill; and to the staff of the Royal Archives.

I am indebted to the Marquis of Salisbury for his kind permission to make use of the papers of the third Marquis at Christ Church, Oxford.

I should also like to thank Dr J. F. A. Mason, the Librarian of Christ Church, who has been most kind and helpful.

Extracts from letters in the Hughenden Archives are published by kind permission of the National Trust, the owners of the copyright. I am most grateful to Mr Rogers and his colleagues for the help that they have given me on my visits to Hughenden Manor.

Extracts from Crown Copyright Records in the Public Record Office appear by kind permission of the Controller of Her Majesty's Stationery Office.

Finally I should like to thank Mr Robert Blake of Christ Church, Oxford, Dr F. R. Bridge of the London School of Economics, and Dr H. G. Roseveare of King's College, London, for valuable help kindly given on various occasions, and the editors of the *Historical Journal*, *History* and *Grundbegriffe der Geschichte* (Gütersloh,

1964) for permission to incorporate in this book in a revised form material that has appeared in their pages.

C. H.

Introduction

THAT Britain's conduct of her relations with other powers was formerly, and more especially during the nineteenth century and at the beginning of the twentieth, governed by a principle, policy or attitude, often described as 'traditional' or 'time-honoured', of 'isolation' — even of 'splendid isolation' — has been the view of many historians. Thus in 1927 the editors of *British Documents on the Origins of the War* referred to Britain's 'traditional principle of "splendid isolation" '.[1] In 1931 the Viennese historian A. F. Pribram wrote of 'the policy of splendid isolation which had been her [Britain's] course for so many years'.[2] In 1948 a Dutch historian, Dr F. Gosses, analysed at some length what he called 'the time-honoured British policy of "splendid isolation" '.[3] Both Pribram and Dr Gosses associated this policy more especially with Salisbury.[4] It would be easy to quote other examples of what is clearly a widely held view.

Indeed, it would be interesting to know who was the first historian, as distinct from contemporary observer, to express this view in print. This is, of course, a matter concerning which it is difficult to speak with certainty. There is a reference in H. E. Egerton's *British Foreign Policy in Europe*, published in 1917, to the dangers to Britain at the end of the nineteenth century of ' "isolation", however "splendid" ',[5] but that is not quite the same thing as the view commonly expressed. In fact, it seems probable that the first historian to put forward

what has since become such a widely accepted view was
William Harbutt Dawson, who in Volume III of the
Cambridge History of British Foreign Policy, published in
1923, referred to 'the old national attitude of "splendid
isolation" ', for which, he claimed, Salisbury had a
'preference'.[6] It is understandable that an opinion expressed in so well known a work of reference should have
exerted much influence on subsequent writers.

   Nevertheless, 'isolation', with or without the epithet
'splendid', is a term concerning which there has been
much disagreement. Was Britain's 'isolation' really an
attitude — even a policy? Or was it merely an embarrassing but entirely involuntary situation in which she
happened to find herself? From whom was Britain
supposedly isolated? Was it simply from the other great
powers of Europe? If not, from whom? Was 'isolation'
Britain's characteristic position during a considerable or
even the greater part of the nineteenth century, or one of
which it would be incorrect to speak with reference to any
period before the closing years of that century? In short,
was Britain's 'isolation' as 'traditional' as it is often stated
to have been? Was Britain's 'isolation' something for
which Salisbury should be regarded as especially responsible, or has his partiality in this respect been exaggerated?
When did Britain's 'isolation' come to an end? Finally,
what, if anything, is the significance in this connexion of
the adjective 'splendid'?

   Various answers have been given to these questions.
The view that 'isolation' was a deliberate policy has been
maintained by numerous historians. On the other hand,
the late Dame Lillian Penson held that 'in so far as Britain
was isolated . . . her isolation was a fact rather than a
policy'; the so-called 'policy of isolation' was, she main-

tained, no more than a 'legend'.[7] Those writers who favour the term 'isolation' usually employ it to describe Britain's attitude towards other powers in general. According to Mr A. J. P. Taylor, however: 'Isolation meant aloofness from the European Balance of Power.'[8] 'Isolation' is frequently referred to as a 'traditional', even a 'time honoured' policy;[9] Professor Hajo Holborn considers that it went back to the eighteen-sixties;[10] Professor Hans Herzfeld to 1815.[11] Mr Taylor holds that it began on 9 July 1894, the day that marked the end of Anglo-Austrian co-operation against Russia — 'a historic date'.[12] The widely held view that Salisbury had a fondness for 'isolation' has been contested by that statesman's own daughter and distinguished biographer, Lady Gwendolen Cecil.[13] The conclusion of the alliance with Japan on 30 January 1902 is usually regarded as marking the end of Britain's 'isolation'.[14] This opinion has also been challenged by Mr Taylor. 'The alliance', he writes, 'did not mark the end of British isolation; rather it confirmed it.'[15] As for 'splendid isolation', it has been dismissed by a recent writer, Dr Zara Steiner, as a 'misleading guide'[16] and 'a cliché which must be abandoned'.[17]

No one would deny that 'splendid isolation' is a cliché, which should be used sparingly. Nevertheless, it should not be assumed that this phrase is one coined by some historian, writing years after the events to which it is supposed to refer. On the contrary, in the last half-decade of the nineteenth century and the first two years of the twentieth — that is, approximately, during Salisbury's third and last administration — 'splendid isolation' was a phrase that was in constant use. It was employed in public speeches by many of the leading politicians of the day, including Salisbury himself, Rosebery, Joseph

B

Chamberlain, Goschen, Harcourt, and John Morley, in debates in the House of Commons, in ambassadorial dispatches and in innumerable articles in newspapers and reviews. It found favour with the Kaiser. All that is not, of course, to say that 'splendid isolation' was a precise term that was conducive to clear and logical thinking concerning Britain's international position and foreign policy.

The purpose of this study is to show how it was that towards the end of the nineteenth century it came to be commonly said that Britain's international position was one of 'isolation'; when, why and in what circumstances this 'isolation' was first described as 'splendid'; how the belief arose that Britain's 'isolation' was a deliberate, indeed a 'traditional', policy; how far this widespread belief corresponded with reality; when and why the wisdom of the continuance of this alleged policy became a subject of controversy; how the belief, shared by so many historians, that Salisbury had a fondness for 'splendid isolation' originated; how far this belief can be justified in the light of Salisbury's own speeches and correspondence and his handling of foreign affairs and more especially of the various proposals made during his administrations of 1886–92 and 1895–1902 for closer links with one or other of the continental powers; and finally, when, in the opinion of contemporaries, Britain's 'isolation, splendid or otherwise', came to an end.

I have chosen the title *Splendid Isolation* for this book only after some hesitation. It is not possible to discuss 'splendid isolation' without also considering 'isolation' *tout court*. 'Isolation', however, is not a term that is exclusively applicable either to Britain or to the period during which Salisbury directed her foreign policy;

'isolation' has been experienced by numerous countries at many different periods. 'Splendid isolation', on the other hand, is a phrase that is appropriate only to Britain; it was coined, caught the popular imagination, and enjoyed its greatest vogue during Salisbury's later years. It is with ideas concerning Britain's international position and foreign policy during those years that this book is primarily, although not exclusively, concerned. On the other hand, some of the ideas that are discussed in the pages that follow go back to a period considerably anterior to 'the later years of the third Marquis of Salisbury', indeed, to a period to which it would be wholly anachronistic to apply the term 'splendid isolation'. I hope to deal with the earlier history of these ideas in a future publication.

Two small problems that have arisen in connexion with the writing of this book should be mentioned. The first concerns the use of the words 'England' and 'English', which it was formerly customary to employ where we should today say or write 'Britain' and 'British'. I have followed modern usage, except, of course, in quotations. The second problem concerns the two Earls of Derby, who are liable to be confused. Edward Stanley (1799–1869), the fourteenth Earl, was three times Prime Minister. I have referred to him throughout as 'the fourteenth Earl of Derby'. His son, Edward Henry Stanley (1826–93), known as Lord Stanley from 1851 to 1869, when he succeeded to the title as fifteenth earl, was Foreign Secretary from 1866 to 1868 and from 1874 to 1878. I have, of course, referred to him as 'Stanley' down to 1869. Thereafter, in view of the fact that I have had occasion to mention him far more often than his father, I have referred to him simply as 'Derby'.

1 Britain's Consciousness of 'Isolation'

BOTH 'isolation' and 'isolate' are words that have come to form part of the English language only in comparatively modern times. Examples of their use in the eighteenth century are rare. When Dr Johnson wished to express the view that the House of Hanover lacked friends in England, he did not say that it was 'isolated'. He said: 'Sir, this Hanoverian family is *isolée* here.'[1] Both 'isolation' and 'isolate' came, however, to be generally accepted in the course of the following century.

In the nineteenth century the normal meaning of the word 'isolation', when employed in an international context, was, as it still is, an embarrassing lack of friends among other powers on whom reliance could be placed for support in case of need. 'Isolation' implied, as it still usually implies, weakness — a dangerous state of affairs, which it was a government's duty to prevent from occurring. On a number of occasions British ministers had been accused of failure in this respect. In 1852, for example, after the dismissal of Palmerston, Clarendon had written to Russell, observing that 'on the day that P. left office' Britain was 'rapidly drifting towards isolation'.[2] In 1864 Gathorne-Hardy, in a speech delivered during the great debate in the House of Commons that followed the Schleswig-Holstein fiasco, had deplored the fact that Britain 'should occupy so isolated a position in the councils of Europe'.[3] In 1885, during the closing months

of Gladstone's second administration, Salisbury had
declared in the House of Lords: 'In Europe we are
isolated; and that boasted Concert of Europe, of which
we used to hear so much, now appears to be a Concert of
Europe against England.'[4] It would be easy to multiply
examples of such remarks. Nevertheless, it was not until
the winter of 1895-6, with its succession of blows to her
prestige in both hemispheres, that Britain's alleged
'isolation' became a catchword — a cliché of the press, of
ambassadorial dispatches and of political speeches.

From 1893 — that is from the second year of Gladstone's final administration — a series of events had
served to emphasize Britain's solitary international
position. In October of that year the visit of the Russian
fleet to Toulon and the demonstrative welcome that it
received had been rightly regarded as proof of a *rapproche-
ment* between two rival naval powers, with unpleasant
implications for Britain's position in the Mediterranean.
In August 1894 a treaty between Britain and the Congo
(at that time a theoretically independent state) for the
exchange by lease of territories in central Africa had had
to be abandoned under pressure from France and
Germany. Meanwhile, there were numerous extra-
European issues outstanding between Britain and Germany, such as the British possession of Walfish Bay,
frontier disputes in West Africa and the future of Samoa.
None of these questions was of vital importance, but
cumulatively they caused much irritation in Germany at
what was regarded as British obstruction of legitimate
German aspirations.[5] These colonial disputes were re-
flected in an unedifying Anglo-German press war, which
gradually increased in intensity during the mid-eighteen-
nineties.[6]

On 9 November 1894 Rosebery spoke, as was and is customary for the Prime Minister, at the Lord Mayor's banquet at the Guildhall. He devoted a considerable part of his speech to the Sino-Japanese War, which had broken out three months previously, declaring that Britain would observe an attitude of neutrality and at the same time attempt to bring about a peaceful settlement. 'In this delicate and difficult business,' added Rosebery, 'we have acted hand in hand with Russia, the other Power mainly interested.' He did not mention Germany.[7] This speech was not well received by the German press.[8] The *Hamburgischer Correspondent* was particularly hostile. Britain, it complained, had of late not only neglected to maintain good relations with other powers; she had even inconsiderately thwarted their plans, and had thus almost completely isolated herself: 'Es hat sich dadurch fast vollständig isolirt.'[9] This was an accusation that cut both ways, the reply to which was obvious.

Accordingly, the *Hamburgischer Correspondent*'s remarks were noted by the *Standard*,[10] a Conservative newspaper, the views of which were regarded as important at this period, especially on the Continent, because of the connexion that Salisbury was known to have with it.[11] (The connecting-link was the *Standard*'s leader-writer, Alfred Austin, whom Salisbury later appointed Poet Laureate in succession to Tennyson, and the connexion was one that Salisbury was himself at pains to minimize.[12]) A few days later the *Standard* replied to the *Hamburgischer Correspondent* in a leading article, which asked rhetorically: 'Is Germany taking the p[lace] so long occupied by France as the "isolated" Power in Europe?' After observing that it had become difficult to know which countries Germany regarded as her friends and which as her foes, the *Standard* concluded condescendingly: 'It is easier for a nation to make enemies than friends, and we should be sorry to see Germany, through want of prudence, land itself in a position of political isolation.'[13]

This retort found its mark. The *Hamburgischer Correspondent* returned to the fray[14] and the *Kölnische Zeitung*, a newspaper particularly subject to the influence of the Press Bureau of the Foreign Ministry,[15] replied to the *Standard* in detail and at length.[16] Numerous other newspapers reacted similarly.[17] Official circles in Germany were also unable to ignore the *Standard*. On 8 December 1894 Sir Edward Malet, the British ambassador in Berlin, reported to Kimberley a conversation with Marschall von Bieberstein, the Secretary of State at the Foreign Ministry, who, said Malet, 'attributed the violence of the German press to the extreme irritation caused by the article in the Standard on the isolation of Germany'. 'I have no doubt', added Malet, 'that this is in a great measure true. The article was like putting a finger into a secret wound that Germany felt but hoped to keep concealed.'[18] A few months later, after Salisbury had returned to the Foreign Office, Malet reverted to this theme: 'The thing of all others that stung them the most was an article in the Standard on the isolation of Germany. The kernel of truth was extremely bitter to them.'[19]

Not surprisingly the Kaiser was unable to resist joining in the argument. On 15 November 1894 Colonel Leopold Swaine, the British military attaché in Berlin and the Englishman to whom at this period he seems to have found it easiest to speak freely, reported that the Kaiser had warned him that, if Britain did not settle her position in the Mediterranean with Austria and Italy, 'she would find herself isolated'.[20] Two months later, on 16 January

1895, Malet reported a conversation, in the course of which the Kaiser asked: 'How do you account for Lord Rosebery's speech at the Guildhall, and the articles even in Conservative papers about the isolation of Germany?'[21] Thus by the beginning of 1895 the Anglo-German argument as to who was really 'isolated' was being conducted at the highest level.

During the first half of 1895 two further events served to differentiate Britain's diplomatic position from that of the other powers. In April Rosebery's government stood aside when Russia, France and Germany intervened in the Far East to compel Japan to modify the terms of the Treaty of Shimonoseki, which, after a brief and spectacularly successful war, she had just imposed on China. This episode prompted Queen Victoria to write to Kimberley: 'The Queen thinks it would be so unfortunate if we found ourselves entirely isolated. . . . She thinks we should not abandon the hope and possibility of trying to do something to avoid our standing entirely aloof.'[22] On 10 June the French foreign minister, Gabriel Hanotaux, speaking in the Chamber of Deputies, to all intents and purposes avowed the existence of an alliance between his country and Russia — an avowal that did not escape the notice of the London press.[23] Britain was now the only great European power that was not a member of one or other of the great alliances, which included Germany, Austria and Italy on the one hand, France and Russia on the other.

The change of government in Britain at the end of June 1895, when Rosebery resigned and Salisbury resumed the prime-ministership and once again took charge of the Foreign Office, brought no immediate improvement in Anglo-German relations. On the contrary, on the very day, 5 August 1895, when the Kaiser in his yacht *Hohenzollern* reached Cowes for what was then his annual visit for the regatta, another wantonly tactless article appeared in the *Standard*, on this occasion aimed at the Kaiser himself: 'We cannot refrain from saying that occasionally there has been exhibited in the Imperial policy a somewhat too strong tendency to try diplomatic experiments.'[24] The pompous lecturing tone of the *Standard*'s article gave renewed offence in Germany[25] and provoked more angry replies in a large number of newspapers.[26] The Kaiser's annoyance was intense and lasted for a considerable time.[27] (The visit to Cowes in 1895 was also the occasion of Salisbury's failure to keep an appointment with the Kaiser on board the *Hohenzollern* on 6 August. Contrary to what has often been stated in the past, however, this episode does not appear to have been a significant cause of the deterioration of the relations between Salisbury and the Emperor.[28])

During the summer of 1895 the Kaiser also developed a suspicion that Salisbury had designs for the partition of the Ottoman Empire, and on 29 August he entertained Swaine to dinner at the palace at Potsdam and explained to the attaché, who was astonished to find himself the only guest, his views on the Eastern Question.[29] In October he took exception to some remarks concerning the situation in South Africa, which had been reported to him as having been made by Malet at a dinner given in his honour at the Wilhelmstrasse on the eve of his retirement from the Berlin embassy. On 25 October, after Malet's departure, he had another conversation with Swaine, complaining forcefully about the language alleged to have been used by Malet and declaring that, as a result of her 'policy of selfishness and bullying', Britain was in a

position of complete 'isolement'. She could only escape
from this situation by taking sides either for or against the
Triple Alliance.[30]

In view of all the unfriendly newspaper exchanges that
had been occurring, it is not surprising that the strongly
worded message to Congress of 17 December 1895 from
the President of the United States, Grover Cleveland, in
connexion with the long-standing dispute between
Britain and Venezuela over the frontier of British Guiana,
was greeted by a section of the German press as proof of
the fact that the 'isolated power' in Europe was really
Britain, and, as was the custom at this period, extracts
from the more acrid articles on this theme were reported
back to London and prominently printed in the leading
British newspapers.[31] On 20 December the Kaiser again
spoke to Swaine, and, according to the latter's memorandum of the conversation, declared: 'There is no question
about it, the newspapers are right in saying: England is
isolated.' After a vigorous complaint about British policy
towards Turkey and a scornful reference to Cleveland's
'monstrous Message to Congress', the Kaiser concluded:
'Now, you have got your hands full and everywhere you
stand alone. Will you be able to continue to do this? Dis-
trust in your aims is the root of all the evil, for you have
made us feel as if we were sitting on a volcano.'[32]

Less than a fortnight after the delivery of Grover
Cleveland's 'monstrous Message to Congress' Dr Jameson
started on his futile raid into the South African Republic,
and on 3 January 1896 the Kaiser dispatched his famous
congratulatory telegram to President Kruger. More
comments on Britain's 'isolation' appeared in the press,
not only of Germany, but of several other countries,
including Austria, Italy and Russia, and once again the

more disagreeable comments were faithfully reproduced in the columns of the principal British newspapers.[33] Salisbury relieved his feelings in a conversation with Count Deym, the Austro-Hungarian ambassador, in which he dwelt at length on the subject that the German newspapers had so repeatedly emphasized — 'die von den deutschen Zeitungen wiederholt betonte Isolierung Englands'.[34]

Highly placed German functionaries, including Hohenlohe, the Imperial Chancellor; Marschall von Bieberstein; Philipp zu Eulenburg, the ambassador in Vienna and the Kaiser's closest friend; and, at a lower level, the industrious Friedrich von Holstein, whom Malet, with considerable discernment, described in a letter to Rosebery as 'the would be "cheville ouvrière" ' of the German Foreign Ministry,[35] dutifully performed variations on the same theme.[36] Indeed, it is probable that the constant harping at this period by the Kaiser and by his ministers and diplomats on the theme of Britain's 'isolation', although to some extent a retort to the offending articles in the *Standard*, was also part of a plan to impress on Britain the weakness of her international position and thus draw her into Germany's diplomatic orbit. Salisbury declined to be influenced by these tactics. On 12 January 1896, the day following what had evidently been a tiresome interview with Hatzfeldt, the German ambassador in London, he wrote to Queen Victoria:

Count Hatzfeldt's language, especially yesterday, supports the idea that the Emperor has really been trying, during the last six months, to frighten England into joining the Triple Alliance. . . . Count Hatzfeldt now wants a secret engagement signed by Lord Salisbury, and three or four of his colleagues; and he enforced this view yesterday in many warnings of the danger of isolation.[37]

The Queen was inclined to take Hatzfeldt's warning seriously. She could not help feeling, she wrote to Salisbury on 14 January, that 'our *isolation* is dangerous'.[38] Salisbury, however, preserved his *sang froid*.

By the middle of the second week of January 1896 no member of the British public who took the trouble to read the newspapers could have failed to be aware that the diplomatic position of his country was one of 'isolation' — at least in the opinion of a large proportion of the world's journalists. In fact, in so far as it is possible to measure such matters, it is probably true to say that there was more talk of Britain's 'isolation' in 1895 and 1896 than at any other time in the nineteenth century or the early twentieth — more, for example, than during the South African War of 1899–1902, with which the term has been associated by so many historians. During that war people in Britain were certainly made unpleasantly conscious of the unpopularity of their country with the press and general public in many parts of the world, and especially in France and Germany. But that is not quite the same thing as 'isolation'. Even at the worst periods of the war in South Africa the difficulties of the British government were not increased by any hostile presidential messages or imperial telegrams.

It is, of course, undeniable that Britain's international position at this time was uncomfortable. Quite apart from her difficulties with the United States and with Germany and the coolness of her relations with France, she had an as yet uncompleted war in Ashanti on her hands. Moreover, Salisbury's efforts, of which his speech at the Guildhall on 11 November 1895 was the one that attracted most attention, to obtain some relief for the unfortunate Armenian subjects of the Ottoman Empire were proving

ineffective, and, precisely because Britain had taken the
lead in seeking a solution for the problem, exposing her
to special humiliation at the hands of the 'unspeakable
Turk'.[39] 'The Powers', recorded Sir Edward Hamilton,
Gladstone's former private secretary, in his diary on 30
December 1895, 'appear to be . . . completely outwitted
by the Sultan. They are in an ignominious position: and
we have a special share of the ignominy.'[40]

The difficulties of Britain's position were generally
apparent. 'We seem nicely hated everywhere,' noted
Gladstone's daughter, Mary Drew, on 8 January 1896.[41]
The following day yet another diarist, Wilfrid Scawen
Blunt, summarized the situation comprehensively: 'We
have now managed in the last six months to quarrel
violently with China, Turkey, Belgium, Ashanti, France,
Venezuela, America and Germany.'[42] 'We have no
friends and no nation loves us,' wrote the military expert,
Spenser Wilkinson.[43] When the new session of Parliament opened on 11 February 1896 the customary reference
to the continuance of friendly relations with other
powers was absent from the Queen's Speech. Instead,
Parliament was told: 'I continue to receive from other
Powers assurances of their friendly sentiments.'[44]

Nevertheless, it soon came to be realized that much that
had been said and written concerning Britain's international difficulties had been exaggerated or tendentious
or both. Some of the articles in the German press clearly
contained an element of propaganda, although it is not
easy to estimate how much of this was officially inspired.
Two contemporary observers, Herbert Bismarck, who
was a friend of Rosebery, and Valentine Chirol, the *Times*
correspondent in Berlin, who kept Salisbury informed
concerning matters about which he had special know-

ledge, both put the blame for the anti-British articles on the German government, or more precisely, in the case of Chirol, on the Press Bureau of the German Foreign Ministry.[45] In fact, there seems to be good reason to believe that the most bitterly anti-British newspapers in Germany were actually those least subject to official influence. It is significant that at the end of 1894 Malet criticized the German government, not for inspiring press attacks on Britain, but for failing to prevent such attacks from being made by the colonial party.[46]

As for the Kaiser's telegram to Kruger, it certainly did not constitute, as so many continental journalists alleged at the time, the final proof of Britain's 'isolation'. Its recognition of the independence of the South African Republic was not imitated by other powers. Indeed, the telegram was coolly received by the Transvaal government. Rosebery thought that Kruger had snubbed the Kaiser and that he did not welcome German interference in his country's affairs: 'He only wishes to be left alone.'[47] The telegram was not followed by any effective action on the part of Germany. Instead, the Kaiser wrote a somewhat lame letter of explanation to his grandmother at Windsor,[48] and, on 3 March 1896, exactly two months after the dispatch of the famous telegram, astonished Berlin by paying a lengthy call on Malet's successor at the British Embassy, Sir Frank Lascelles. Lascelles attributed the Kaiser's visit to his realization that any sort of alliance between Germany and Russia had become an impossibility, and commented on the weakening of the Triple Alliance that had resulted from Italy's recent misadventures in Africa. There was no doubt, wrote Lascelles, that the Kaiser now sincerely desired friendly relations with Britain. It does not appear that there was any further allusion on the occasion of this visit to the 'isolation' either of Britain or of Germany.[49]

Moreover, not all the powers had displayed hostility. From Paris the British ambassador, Dufferin and Ava, wrote to Queen Victoria on New Year's Day, 1896, pointing out that although people in France would have been glad to see Britain entangled in a quarrel with the United States, they recognized that Grover Cleveland's interpretation of the Monroe Doctrine was also inimical to the interests of France.[50] Russia made no move. Italy, whose army had just suffered one defeat in Ethiopia and was about to suffer another and more disastrous one, was in no position to make unfriendly gestures at anyone. As for Austria–Hungary, it was obvious that the Kruger telegram had occasioned embarrassment in Vienna, where the government did its best quietly to dissociate the Dual Monarchy from the action of its German ally.[51] Meanwhile, the Canadian government showed its appreciation of the need for military preparedness in case of war with the United States,[52] and in Australia the Prime Ministers of all the colonies publicly assured Salisbury of their loyal support and of their determination 'to resent interference in matters of British and colonial concern.[53]

In London the policy of the government was marked by a combination of public valour and diplomatic discretion. The Admiralty's announcement on 9 January 1896 of the commissioning of the 'Flying Squadron' sounded a defiant note. On the other hand, on 11 January the Cabinet prudently decided to negotiate with the United States with a view to a settlement of the dispute with Venezuela.[54] On 16 January an agreement concerning Siam was signed with France, apropos of which Salisbury wrote to the Queen: 'It was felt to be important in the present state of things to settle as many questions with France as possible.'[55] Within a comparatively short time public tension relaxed. Britain's 'isolation' was dismissed by the *Standard* as an 'empty phrase'[56] and by the *Morning Post* as 'imaginary'.[57] On 21 January Hatzfeldt himself reported home on the lack of concern in Britain at the country's alleged 'isolation', about which, he added, people actually boasted.[58]

Nevertheless, although Britain's 'isolation' might be dismissed as 'imaginary', one lesson of the events of 1895–6 was plain to those able to judge. The government's decisions first to negotiate with Washington and eventually to agree to submit all the territory in dispute with Venezuela to arbitration constituted an acquiescence in a very broad interpretation of the Monroe Doctrine. Kimberley saw this when, in a letter to Rosebery, he observed: 'The recognition of the quasi U.S. Protectorate over the whole of America (which is the obvious result of admitting their claim to interfere in our quarrel with Venezuela) is a step which must have far-reaching consequences.'[59] Rosebery thought that 'as between Salisbury and Olney [the United States Secretary of State] the victory must be held to rest almost entirely with the latter', and that 'the admission of the Monroe doctrine in its most extreme form appears to be complete'.[60] The fact was that Britain could not afford to become involved in a quarrel with the United States, at least in the western hemisphere. No doubt the recognition of this situation was in the long run salutary. Kimberley saw that the admission of the United States' claim would not be to Britain's disadvantage.[61]

c

2 'Splendid but Dangerous Isolation'

IT was on 16 January 1896, just over a month after the delivery of Grover Cleveland's message to Congress and almost a fortnight after the dispatch of the Kaiser's telegram to President Kruger, that Britain's 'isolation', about which so much had been said and written, was for the first time dignified by the addition of the adjective 'splendid'. 'Splendid isolation' is a phrase of Canadian origin. Its real author, although he was not the first person to utter these precise words, was George Eulas Foster, leader of the Canadian House of Commons and Minister of Finance in the Conservative government of Sir Mackenzie Bowell. On the day in question Foster was speaking in the debate on the address in reply to the speech from the throne, and the words that he actually used were: 'The great mother Empire stands splendidly isolated in Europe.'[1]

The first recorded example of the use of the phrase in the form in which it is almost invariably quoted, however, appears to have occurred in the course of a speech by Sir Richard Cartwright, a prominent member of the Canadian Liberal Party. Later in the debate on 16 January Cartwright paraphrased Foster's remark concerning Britain's position by way of expressing his disagreement: 'I have a word or two to say on this same subject of "splendid isolation".' He dismissed Foster's observation as 'grandiloquent nonsense', and declared: 'England does stand isolated, but I think true statesmen would have said that

England stands dangerously isolated, and not splendidly isolated.'[2]

Neither Foster's words nor Cartwright's paraphrase of them made, so far as one can judge from the absence of press comment, much immediate impression in Canada. But Foster's speech was reported in the London *Times*[3] and quoted — or, rather, slightly misquoted — by Joseph Chamberlain in the course of a speech at a banquet in honour of a new governor of Queensland on 21 January 1896. 'Three weeks ago,' declared Chamberlain, 'in the words of Mr Foster, the leader of the House of Commons of the Dominion of Canada, "the great mother-Empire stood splendidly isolated".'[4] The paragraph of which this sentence formed part was printed in *The Times* under the cross-heading 'Splendid Isolation', and this phrase was also given prominence in other leading newspapers.[5] 'Splendid isolation' was already on its way to becoming a stock, although a generally unacknowledged, quotation.

How was it that on 16 January 1896 eminent Canadian statesmen were arguing, not without some heat, about whether Britain's 'isolation', as to the fact of which they were agreed, was 'splendid' or 'dangerous'? The Cleveland message had disturbed Canadians, who could not but be aware of the unpleasant consequences for themselves that a war between Britain and the United States would entail. Mackenzie Bowell's government accordingly took immediate steps to strengthen the country's defences,[6] to which the speech from the throne drew the attention of the dominion parliament, when it reassembled on 2 January 1896.[7] The days that followed saw the dispatch of the Kruger telegram, the commissioning of the 'Flying Squadron' and the loyal message from the Prime Ministers of the Australian colonies.[8] Meanwhile, Canadian newspapers reported the more spiteful continental press comments on Britain's diplomatic position,[9] and themselves proffered observations to the same effect. 'She [Britain] is practically isolated', remarked the Toronto *Globe* on 15 January, 'so far as European sympathy is concerned.'[10] Preparedness, imperial solidarity and the mother country's exposed diplomatic position were accordingly all topics of the hour, when, on 16 January 1896, the address in reply to the speech from the throne was debated in the Canadian House of Commons, and Foster uttered the words that, although in a modified form, were destined to become historic.

On the same day notice was given of a motion assuring the British government, in view of the threatening international situation, of the House's loyalty to the British throne and its conviction that, should the occasion arise, in no other part of the Empire would more substantial sacrifices attest the determination of the Queen's subjects to maintain the integrity of the Empire than in Canada, but also expressing the desire of the people of Canada to maintain the most friendly relations with the United States.[11] The debate on this motion took place on 5 February 1896, when the question whether Britain's 'isolation' was 'splendid' or 'dangerous' was eloquently and exhaustively discussed in an atmosphere of patriotic solidarity.[12] On this occasion, when party differences were temporarily effaced, Cartwright offered a compromise on the issue concerning which he and Foster had previously disagreed. 'We shall say in future,' he declared, 'not that England stands in a state of splendid isolation, or of dangerous isolation, but that England stands in a state of splendid but dangerous isolation.'[13]

What precisely did those Canadians mean, who in the

early months of 1896 declared that Britain was in a position of 'splendid isolation'? So far as the second half of the phrase is concerned, the answer is simple. Britain was isolated in that she was the target of hostile gestures by foreign governments, and lacked, not merely allies, but friends among the great powers. The Toronto *Globe* wrote that Britain was 'in the position of a power isolated and threatened with loss and humiliation'.[14] There was no suggestion in the debates in the Canadian House of Commons, either on 16 January or on 5 February, that Britain's 'isolation' was a deliberate policy.

The question of the significance of the adjective 'splendid' as a description of this 'isolation' cannot be answered so simply.

Primarily, of course, it was an expression of the complacency, so characteristic of the period, concerning Britain's position as, in the words of W. S. Gilbert, 'the greatest, the most powerful, the wisest country in the world'.[15] Foster referred to her 'interests stretching over the wide world' and her 'commerce the greatest of any nation of the world has ever possessed'.[16] This complacency found elaborate expression in a speech by Wilfrid Laurier, the leader of the Liberal Opposition, during the debate of 5 February 1896. After referring to the contentious question whether Britain — or rather, to be strictly accurate, England — was 'splendidly isolated or dangerously isolated', he concluded:

For my part, I think splendidly isolated, because this isolation of England comes from her superiority, and her superiority today seems to be manifest. Apart from the realm of letters and art — in which, in my humble judgment, France is her compeer, and even her superior — in everything that makes a people great, in colonizing power, in trade and commerce, in all the higher arts of civilization,

England not only excels all other nations of the modern world, but all nations in ancient history as well.[17]

Others who professed their belief in the splendour of Britain's 'isolation' probably took her superiority — more especially her naval superiority — for granted, without bothering to justify it at such length.

But for some the epithet 'splendid' had another and less obvious implication. It expressed the assurance that in her international difficulties, which had so conspicuously multiplied recently, Britain could always rely on the loyal support of her self-governing colonies. Of such support there had been examples just over a decade previously. In 1884 Wolseley had recruited Canadian *voyageurs* for service as civilian auxiliaries on the Nile campaign for the relief of Gordon. After the fall of Khartoum the New South Wales government had raised a contingent of some seven hundred men for service in Africa. In the debate on 16 January Foster, after alluding to the 'splendidly isolated' position of the 'great mother Empire', went on to emphasize that Britain's 'pride and glory must base itself upon the strong arms and willing loyal hearts of the citizenship of that Empire from one end of it to the other'.[18] In the debate on 5 February this theme was developed further. One Liberal orator declared that 'the hearts of her children have gone out to the great lone, isolated mother',[19] and Laurier told the House: 'If the day should come — which God forbid — if the day should ever come — which I again say God forbid — when England should have to repel foes, I am quite sure that all British subjects, all over the world, would be only too glad to give her what help they could.'[20] These assurances of colonial support for Britain in case of need were not vain ones, as events little more than three years later were to prove.

It is, moreover, no accident that the phrase 'splendid isolation' became popular in Britain partly as the result of a speech on a highly imperial occasion by the Colonial Secretary, Joseph Chamberlain, then enjoying, as the result of his handling of events during and after the Jameson Raid, prestige and popularity greater than he had even known before. *The Times* next day reported his speech under the headline: 'Mr Chamberlain on Colonial Loyalty',[21] and later in the week the *Spectator* observed that 'the Colonies think our isolation "splendid", for in direct proportion to our isolation is both our power to serve them, and our disposition to lean on them in case we ourselves get into a quarrel with other States'.[22] Perhaps the point was most forcefully put, once again by Chamberlain, in a speech delivered nearly six years later, after a retort that he had made to criticisms of the British Army's conduct of the war in South Africa had excited a storm of indignation in Germany. On 6 January 1902 Chamberlain declared at Birmingham: 'We have the feeling, unfortunately, that we have to count upon ourselves alone, and I say, therefore, it is the duty of the British people to count upon themselves alone, as their ancestors did. I say alone, yes, in a splendid isolation, surrounded and supported by our kinsfolk.'[23]

Of course, not everyone who spoke or wrote of Britain's 'splendid isolation' did so with these implications in mind. The phrase never had a precise and universally accepted meaning. Its popularity soon resulted in its acquiring a variety of meanings. It lent itself to irony and was often so employed, especially, of course, by the government's Liberal critics and by observers abroad, including the Kaiser, who had a weakness for journalistic phraseology.[24] It was with much justice that a

French journalist observed towards the end of 1896: ' "Splendid isolation" is neither more nor less than one of those hollow, resounding, dangerous phrases such as "L'Empire, c'est la paix", or "masterly inactivity", or "Peace with honour", with which people let themselves be deluded.'[25] Nevertheless, 'splendid isolation' was a phrase that evidently expressed the feelings of a great many people at the time when it caught the popular imagination. It would not otherwise have gained such wide currency.

3 'Isolation' as a Policy

THE idea that 'isolation' might be, not merely an involuntary position of weakness, but also a deliberate policy goes back in Britain at least to the eighteen-sixties.[1] For a long time, however, 'isolation', even when referred to in this way, was still, nevertheless, a term of disparagement. It usually meant refusal to collaborate in any way with other powers. A policy of 'isolation' was something that one attributed to one's political opponents or against which one advised one's colleagues. In 1871, for example, Gladstone's government was accused in the House of Commons by Sir Robert Peel (the son of the famous Prime Minister) of pursuing a 'policy of isolation — of selfish isolation'.[2] In 1877 Salisbury warned Beaconsfield of the evils that would result from adopting a 'policy of isolation' in regard to the Eastern Question.[3] In the eighteen-sixties and seventies, however, such usage was infrequent. It was during the press campaign of 1895–6, which reached its climax in the days that followed the Kruger telegram, that to refer to Britain's 'isolation' as a matter of policy became for the first time common usage. The *Contemporary Review*, the *Speaker*, the *Spectator* and the *Saturday Review* were among the papers that set the fashion.[4]

At about the same time it also became common to refer to this voluntary 'isolation' on the part of Britain without any of the disparaging implications that the term had usually carried with it hitherto. The outstanding example of this new fashion was a speech to a Conservative audience at Lewes on 26 February 1896 by George Joachim Goschen, the First Lord of the Admiralty in Salisbury's Cabinet and the minister responsible for the creation of the 'Flying Squadron' during the days of tension that had followed the Cleveland Message. 'Much has been said,' Goschen rightly observed, 'with regard to the isolation of England.' He distinguished between what he called 'two kinds of isolation', observing:

There may be the isolation of those who are weak and who therefore are not courted because they can contribute nothing, and there is, on the other hand, the isolation of those who do not wish to be entangled in any complications and will hold themselves free in every respect.

Goschen then went on to declare: 'Our isolation is not an isolation of weakness; it is deliberately chosen, the freedom to act as we choose in any circumstances that may arise.' Thus, claimed Goschen, while other powers were 'bartering favour for favour, promise for promise': 'We have stood alone in that which is called isolation — our splendid isolation, as one of our colonial friends was good enough to call it.'[5]

Goschen's speech, which aroused much comment, probably did more than anything else to spread the notion that Britain's much discussed 'isolation' was both 'deliberately chosen' and 'splendid'. Five days later Rosebery replied to Goschen at length in a speech at the Eighty Club, in which he disputed the wisdom of what he called 'this policy of splendid isolation'.[6] On the same evening John Morley, who had lost his seat in Parliament the previous year and was fighting a by-election in the Montrose Burghs, spoke similarly.[7] On 5 March, after Goschen had introduced the naval estimates — the

highest till then in British history — in the House of
Commons, there took place a prolonged discussion of
Britain's 'splendid isolation', which, declared Dilke, who
had raised the subject, was also 'a necessary isolation'.[8]

It was also, apparently, at about the same period that
the term 'isolation' acquired a new connotation, which
was somewhat narrower than any that it had had hitherto.
In the Commons debate on 5 March 1896 Harcourt
developed the theme of the 'two kinds of isolation',
explaining that there was 'isolation which arises from the
unfriendliness of the world', but also that 'isolation may
be that you have not desired to enter into permanent or
entangling alliances'.[9] (The phrase 'entangling alliances',
employed by Harcourt, was, it may be noted, another
expression that enjoyed great popularity in Britain in the
later nineteenth century. It is, of course, a quotation, also
seldom acknowledged, from Thomas Jefferson's 'First
Inaugural Address', delivered in 1801). A few weeks later
Spenser Wilkinson, in a book entitled *The Nation's
Awakening*, based on a series of articles in the *Morning
Post*, referred to 'that abstinence from alliances which has
lately been glorified under the name of isolation'.[10] From
about this period 'isolation', while, of course, retaining
its earlier connotations, was spoken and written of in-
creasingly frequently in the sense of the systematic
avoidance of any formal alliance with a foreign power.

Of course, 'isolation', with or without the adjective
'splendid', is not and never has been a technical term of
the type that is to be found neatly and authoritatively
defined in reference-books compiled for the use of professional diplomats. Contemporary definitions, such as
those just quoted, are by no means free from ambiguity.
Did a policy of 'isolation' preclude all alliances? Or only

alliances in peace-time? Or only peace-time alliances with great powers? Or only peace-time alliances with the great powers of Europe? One could cite passages from contemporary documents to illustrate each one of these shades of meaning.[11] Nor, as Salisbury on one occasion pointed out,[12] is the word 'alliance' itself at all precise. In the nineteenth century it was often employed to describe relationships between powers far less close and formal than those to which it is usually applied today. There was, moreover, no document that constituted a classic and widely known statement of Britain's policy of 'isolation' in the way that Washington's 'Farewell Address' and Jefferson's 'First Inaugural' did of what came to be known later in the United States as 'isolationism'. Indeed, it would not be easy to say who was the founder of the policy of 'isolation', or when that policy first came into existence, if it ever did so.

Nevertheless, it is significant and can hardly have been a coincidence that talk of Britain's 'isolation' as a matter of deliberate choice became fashionable within a few months of it being generally realized that France and Russia had come together. Britain's detached position was thereby rendered all the more conspicuous. In October 1895 Dufferin and Ava reported from Paris some remarks made to Blowitz, the *Times* correspondent, by Lobanov, the Russian Foreign Minister, who was on a visit to the French capital:

The situation of Europe has naturally drawn us together. Both France and Russia are instinctively social. They are like two travellers along the same road. At first they walk on opposite sides. Then they draw a little nearer together, and begin talking about their mutual concerns. After a little they see three other people walking in the same direction, linked arm in arm. This suspicious attitude brings the two acquaintances into still closer contact, and they also link arms. England is the only Nation that is content to remain in isolation, and the only Nation whose position permits such an attitude. She likes it, and she is proud of it.[13]

Had it not been for her aloofness from the two groups of travellers, much less would, in all probability, have been heard of Britain's deliberate 'isolation'.

It should not be thought, of course, that it ever became a universal practice to refer to Britain's unwillingness to conclude alliances with other powers as a policy of 'isolation', still less of 'splendid isolation'. Many leading politicians, especially those who most strongly favoured the maintenance of what they regarded as Britain's existing freedom from entanglements, seem deliberately to have avoided making any public declaration that might have suggested pride in their country's isolation. 'I am not one', Campbell-Bannerman told the House of Commons in 1902, 'who thinks it very admirable to boast of our isolation'. Nevertheless, Campbell-Bannerman was a firm believer in the desirability of preserving what he called Britain's 'freedom of individual action'.[14]

4 'Jargon About Isolation'

In 1898 the wisdom of the continuance of Britain's policy of 'isolation' became the subject of a heated controversy.[1]

The autumn of 1897 had seen the beginning of what has often been called 'the scramble for China'. This 'scramble' was, of course, initiated, not by Russia, but by Germany. For some time the German government had been considering the acquisition of a harbour in the Far East. In 1896 Tirpitz, the newly appointed commander of the German squadron in Chinese waters, had reported to Berlin that the most suitable place for such a harbour would be Kiaochow Bay on the Yellow Sea coast of the Chinese province of Shantung. In the following year the German government accordingly took up with Russia the question of the use by Germany of Kiaochow Bay. Then, at the beginning of November 1897, two German missionaries, who had been working in the province of Shantung, were murdered. German troops were landed in Kiaochow Bay on 14 November 1897, and eventually, by an agreement concluded with China on 6 March 1898, Germany acquired the lease of Kiaochow and of the surrounding district for a period of ninety-nine years.

Germany's initiative in the Far East, significant as it may appear in the light of later events, occasioned no great concern in Britain. Germany was not as yet a major naval power and her proceedings on the coast of China were not regarded as a threat to British interests. But her action was quickly followed by that of Russia. In December 1897 the Russian Far Eastern fleet was ordered to proceed to what was then known as Port Arthur, at the tip of the peninsula of Liaotung, which constitutes the southern part of Manchuria. The strategic importance of Port Arthur, commanding, as it does, the entrance to the Gulf of Pechili (Po Hai) and therefore the approaches to Peking, was regarded as considerable. Russia, moreover, was, at least numerically, a great naval power. Accordingly, the arrival at Port Arthur of the Russian fleet caused concern in London, to which was added indignation, when the Russian government asked for and obtained the withdrawal of certain British warships from the area.

Salisbury's reaction to these events was to seek a *modus vivendi* with Russia, not merely in the Far East, but in Asia as a whole. However, nothing came of this approach, and at the beginning of March 1898 the Russian government asked China for a lease both of Port Arthur and of the neighbouring town of Talienwan (Dairen). Chamberlain was unable to take these events as calmly as did the Prime Minister. On 3 February 1898 he wrote to Balfour, warning him that the government would find itself in trouble if it did not pursue a more decided course of action in China, and suggesting that approaches be made to both the United States and to Germany. On 17 March he had a long talk with the Japanese minister in London. No positive response was forthcoming from either the United States or from Japan, and on 25 March the Cabinet met and decided, Chamberlain dissenting, to ask China for a lease of Weihaiwei, on the north coast of Shantung, just across the Strait of Pechili from Port Arthur. The implication of this decision was that no opposition would be offered to Russia in Manchuria itself. Two days later

Russia signed an agreement with China for the lease of
Port Arthur and Talienwan.

The events in Manchuria were widely regarded as
constituting a set-back for Britain, and there was much
criticism of Salisbury in the press. After the Cabinet
meeting on 25 March Salisbury left for a holiday in
France. On 29 March Chamberlain saw Hatzfeldt probably
at the house of Alfred Rothschild, the financier, and in
the course of their conversation he acknowledged, according to his own account, that Britain had for many years had
'a policy of isolation — or at least of non-entanglement
in alliances' and observed that this policy might in the
future have to be changed. There followed, according to
Chamberlain, a discussion of the possibility of an Anglo-
German alliance, based upon a mutual understanding as
to policy in China and elsewhere.[2] Further conversations
followed both with Hatzfeldt and with a certain Baron
von Eckardstein, who at this time was only unofficially
attached to the German Embassy, but had valuable con-
tacts in London society.[3] (He had married the only
daughter and heiress of Sir Blundell Maple, the wealthy
head of the well-known furniture business in Tottenham
Court Road, who was also a Conservative Member of
Parliament and the owner of a string of race-horses.)

On 5 April there was a foreign-affairs debate in the
House of Commons, in the course of which the government was warned against an attitude of 'isolation', and
urged to co-operate in the Far East with other powers.
'We must not', remarked Sir Edward Grey, 'look to
isolation. We must find a common ground of interest
with other Powers.'[4] The independently-minded Conservative, Admiral Lord Charles Beresford, argued that
the time for 'splendid isolation' was past; the government

should try to make an alliance with Germany and Japan.[5] On 4 May Salisbury, having returned from France, and having, it may be presumed, read both the report of this debate and also Chamberlain's memoranda of his conversations with Hatzfeldt, addressed the annual meeting of the Primrose League at the Albert Hall. 'We know', he declared, in what is often called the 'dying nations' speech, 'that we shall maintain against all comers that which we possess, and we know, in spite of the jargon about isolation, that we are amply competent to do so.'[6]

Salisbury's contemptuous dismissal of 'the jargon about isolation' acquired added significance when, nine days later, on 13 May, Chamberlain spoke at Birmingham Town Hall. This speech is also remembered by one of its key phrases. 'I have always thought that it was a very wise proverb,' remarked Chamberlain in a passage directed against Russia, ' "Who sups with the Devil must have a long spoon." ' The speech was important, not only because of its anti-Russian tone, but also for the warning that it gave concerning the 'policy of strict isolation', which, Chamberlain claimed, had been pursued by Britain ever since the Crimean War. After a reference to the alliances of the great continental powers and Britain's liability, as long as she remained outside those alliances, to be confronted at any moment with a hostile combination of other powers, Chamberlain continued:

If the policy of isolation, which has hitherto been the policy of this country, is to be maintained in the future, then the fate of the Chinese Empire may be, probably will be, hereafter decided without reference to our wishes and in defiance of our interests. If . . . we are determined to enforce the policy of the open door . . . we must not reject the idea of an alliance with those Powers whose interests most nearly approximate to our own.[7]

D

The 'long spoon' speech was naturally interpreted as a call for an alliance with Germany.[8] Its reception by the press was by no means universally hostile,[9] but it stirred Liberals in both Houses of Parliament to protest. In the House of Lords Kimberley asked Salisbury on 17 May for an explanation of his colleague's remarks, which implied a challenge to 'the principle upon which we have for many years acted with regard to our foreign affairs, of not engaging in what are commonly called entangling alliances'.[10] Salisbury was unforthcoming. He had not, he explained, a copy with him of the text of Chamberlain's speech.[11] In the House of Commons Dilke raised the matter on 10 June in connexion with the annual Foreign Office vote, defending and attempting, with only limited success, to clarify the policy that, as he saw it, Chamberlain had called in question. 'A policy of isolation', he explained, 'does not, of course, necessarily imply isolation in war. . . . The policy against which I am protesting is that of permanent, standing alliances when war is not in immediate view.'[12] Other leading Liberals who followed Dilke left no doubt that their party was on the side of the existing order. 'I am altogether opposed,' declared Asquith, 'as I believe the vast majority of our people are, to abandoning the free hand in these matters which we have always enjoyed.'[13] Labouchere and Harcourt spoke to similar effect.[14]

When Chamberlain spoke later in the debate he did not, in what was, no doubt, a more critical atmosphere than that of the Birmingham Town Hall, repeat the *ipsissima verba* of his 'long spoon' speech. Nevertheless, he maintained that 'the policy of this country, hitherto well known to all nations of the world, and declared again and again was that we would not accept any alliance'. He had no difficulty in answering Dilke. After all, no one had hitherto suggested forming any 'permanent or standing alliance'.[15] In fact, the 'long spoon' speech, like some of his other utterances, had committed Chamberlain less than at first sight appeared. He had not proposed that the policy of 'isolation' be terminated. He had merely called attention to the probable consequence of its continuance.

There was, in any case, no need for Liberals to fear that Britain was in imminent danger of forfeiting her traditional freedom of action. There was no likelihood of Chamberlain achieving the alliance with Germany to check Russia in the Far East for which he hoped. Salisbury had seen this when he wrote to Chamberlain on 2 May 1898: 'I quite agree with you that under the circumstances a closer relation with Germany would be very desirable; but can we get it?'[16] A few weeks later Lascelles, the ambassador in Berlin, reported to Salisbury a conversation with the Kaiser, who explained unequivocally the insuperable objections to Chamberlain's proposal:

But the report was that the object of the Alliance was that Germany should join England in driving Russia out of China. This of course was out of the question. Germany had not the means of fighting Russia in China, and even if she attempted to do so, Germany herself would be invaded both by Russia and by France, and said His Majesty, 'Where should I be then and how could you help me[?].'[17]

An Anglo-German alliance against Russia was not within the range of practical politics.

Later in the year Chamberlain, in a speech at Wakefield on 8 December, returned to the problems of Britain's imperial concerns and foreign relations:

When I spoke, as I shall speak again, of the splendid isolation of this country, I gave expression to my deep-rooted conviction that the British Empire, by which I mean the United Kingdom and her children across the seas, is well able to defend against all attack its own possessions and its own exclusive interests. That is a task which we will undertake alone, and in its performance we ask for no help and we need no alliances. But there are other interests which are not ours exclusively, which others have with us in common, and surely it is not unreasonable to anticipate that in promoting these interests there shall be a certain amount of co-operation.[18]

It was thus possible to be in favour both of 'splendid isolation' and of co-operation with other powers in defence of common interests.

The following year, 1899, saw another public pronouncement by Chamberlain on the subject of Britain's 'isolation'. In November, only a few weeks after the outbreak of war in South Africa, the Kaiser, accompanied by Bülow, the Secretary of State at the German Foreign Ministry, paid a visit to his grandmother at Windsor. Salisbury, whose wife died on the day of the Kaiser's arrival, did not on this occasion come to Windsor, but Chamberlain was present and had a conversation with the Kaiser on 21 November and with Bülow three days later.[19] On 29 November, after a brief stay at Sandringham, the imperial party left for home. The very next day Chamberlain, who, according to his biographer, was suffering from a heavy cold,[20] spoke at a Unionist luncheon at Leicester and told his audience: 'But there is something more which I think any far-seeing English statesman must have long desired, and that is that we should not remain permanently isolated on the continent of Europe; and I think that the moment that aspiration was formed it must have appeared evident to everybody that the natural alliance is between ourselves and the great German Empire.' The speech also contained a passage on 'a new Triple Alliance between the Teutonic race and the two great branches of the Anglo-Saxon race'.[21] This imprudent utterance, which was also strongly anti-French in tone, was almost everywhere unfavourably received.[22]

On 11 December 1899 Bülow spoke in the Reichstag in support of a new navy bill, stressing Germany's need for a fleet large enough to resist any possible attack. His speech emphasized the importance to Germany of her ties with her partners in the Triple Alliance and of her friendship with Russia. His reference to Britain as a power with whom Germany desired to live in peace and harmony on a basis of full reciprocity and mutual consideration was probably as friendly as any that he could afford to make at the time in view of the strength of anti-British feeling then prevailing in Germany. Chamberlain, in a disgruntled letter to Lascelles, observed that Bülow's speech 'so far as England is concerned is limited to *le plus strict nécessaire*'.[23] Bülow did not, of course, respond in any way to the Leicester overture. Thereafter Chamberlain did not again publicly canvass the desirability of ending Britain's 'isolation' or preach the need for an alliance with any other power.

This *contretemps* did not, of course, mark the end of confidential discussions with a view to terminating Britain's 'isolation'. Eckardstein, now first secretary at the German Embassy, visited Chatsworth in January 1901, and, according to his own account, both Devonshire and Chamberlain, who was also a guest, expressed the view that the time for 'splendid isolation' was over.[24] On 18 March 1901 Eckardstein saw Lansdowne at the Foreign Office.[25] On 23 May Hatzfeldt, according to Lansdowne, reverted to the theme of the danger to Britain of her 'isolement'.[26] Lansdowne's report of this

renewed warning duly reached Salisbury, who commented on it in what is probably his most famous state-
paper, his minute of 29 May 1901. 'Count Hatzfeldt',
wrote Salisbury, 'speaks of our *"isolation"* as constituting a
serious danger for us. *Have we ever felt that danger practically?*'
After an excursus into the history of the revolutionary
and Napoleonic wars, Salisbury continued:

Except during his [Napoleon I's] reign we have never even been in
danger; and, therefore, it is impossible for us to judge whether
the 'isolation' under which we are supposed to suffer, does or does
not contain in it any elements of peril. It would hardly be wise to
incur novel and most onerous obligations, in order to guard against
a danger in whose existence we have no historical reason for believing.[27]

Six months later, Francis Bertie, at that time assistant
under-secretary and head of the Asiatic Section at the
Foreign Office, drafted a memorandum which constituted
an even more elaborate rebuttal of the German argument
that Britain's 'isolation' was a source of danger to her.
'The German Government', he wrote on 9 November
1901, 'lay stress on the danger to England of isolation,
and enlarge on the advantages to her to be secured by an
alliance with Germany. They have constantly and for
some years past made use of these threats and blandishments.' Bertie argued that the experience of the South
African War, when it had not been possible for the other
great powers to combine in demanding that Britain desist
from the war or accept arbitration was 'the best proof
that isolation is not so dangerous as the German Government would have us believe'.[28] There is, as has recently
been pointed out, a marked note of confidence in Britain's
international position discernible in this memorandum,
which may well have been the result of Bertie's knowledge
that an alliance with Japan was in prospect.[29]

5 The 'Traditional Policy'

As understood by Dilke and by many others 'isolation' was, of course, simply a term that it had recently become fashionable to employ to describe what had long been widely regarded as an established principle of British foreign policy. For years past politicians, particularly, but not exclusively, on the Liberal side, had been making speeches insisting on the necessity of preserving Britain's 'free hand' or of avoiding any 'entangling', 'exclusive', 'monopolizing', 'separate', 'single' or 'special' — the epithets varied — alliances with other powers. Public pronouncements to this effect by leading politicians go back to at least the eighteen-forties. In 1866 the fourteenth Earl of Derby had told the House of Lords, shortly after forming his third administration, that it was the British government's duty 'to keep itself upon terms of good-will with all surrounding nations, but not to entangle itself with any single or monopolizing alliance with any one of them'.[1] More recently, on 3 March 1896, Rosebery had declared in a speech to the Eighty Club: 'It is not possible in our conditions, and still less is it desirable, to enter into a system of alliances.'[2] Suaver explanations of the same point by successive Foreign Secretaries in interviews with ambassadors and in dispatches go back to a period that it would be rash to specify.[3] Occasionally, it occurred to someone to point out that the principle only held good in peace-time and when war was not an immediate danger.[4]

The arguments adduced in support of this principle were various. Salisbury emphasized the advantage to Britain of her 'insular position which makes the burdensome conditions of an alliance unnecessary' and — this was the argument that he employed most frequently — the attitude prescribed by her 'popular constitution'.[5] Harcourt stressed the perils of involvement in the affairs of great military despotisms and Britain's status as a great naval power.[6] Kimberley pointed out that even a defensive alliance was necessarily directed against some other power.[7] Asquith claimed that alliances were repugnant to the British people.[8] Perhaps the argument that was used most frequently, however, particularly by successive Foreign Secretaries and by British ambassadors abroad, was the appeal to established practice. The avoidance of alliances was Britain's 'traditional policy'. Thus in 1901 Lascelles reported having reminded the Kaiser of the British government's 'traditional policy of avoiding alliances which would bind them for a long period'.[9]

As to the precise age of this tradition there were differences of opinion and some uncertainty. 'Many years,' said Kimberley in the House of Lords after Chamberlain's 'long spoon' speech.[10] 'Nearly fifty years,' declared Asquith in the Commons a few weeks later.[11] 'Nearly a century,' claimed Harcourt during the Commons debate on the Anglo-Japanese alliance on 13 February 1902.[12] Henry Norman, a Liberal back-bencher, who had earlier opened the debate, asserted that 'the policy of England had always been freedom from alliances'.[13] It is human to over-estimate the antiquity of any principle that one values, and it is probably true to say that, the greater a man's attachment to the 'traditional policy', the more he tended to stress, indeed to exaggerate, its venerability.

Nevertheless, however traditional the policy might be, the pronouncements in its support made in the last years of the nineteenth century and at the beginning of the twentieth had a significance that was absent from similar declarations made a generation earlier. There can be little doubt that to most people in Britain during Salisbury's later years their country's 'free hand' meant above all freedom from the quasi-permanent alliances that had grown up on the Continent since 1879 and in which the other five great powers were all involved — or from anything like them. 'No British Ministry', declared Harcourt at the Eighty Club on 13 April 1897, 'has ever dared to propose to join the Triple Alliance or the Dual Alliance. It has kept a free hand, as England ought always to keep a free hand, for a free people.'[14]

How far was devotion to the 'traditional policy' a characteristic of any one particular party? So far as the Liberals are concerned, the question is a comparatively simple one. Between 1896 and 1902 most of the leading spokesmen of the party, including Rosebery, Kimberley, Harcourt, Campbell-Bannerman and Asquith, publicly proclaimed the undesirability of any formal alliance with any other power. On the other hand, it is clear, and a study of the events of 1902 confirms this, that feeling on the subject was less strong among those who came to be known, not very precisely, as Liberal Imperialists than among those members of the party whose attitude towards foreign policy was closer to the Gladstonian tradition. These nuances of opinion are also visible in the Liberal press.

The Conservative position was more complicated. The fourteenth Earl of Derby's objection to 'any single or monopolizing alliance' has been noted. It does not seem that his words had any durable effect on the outlook of

the party. His son held similar opinions,[15] but he was by
no means a typical Conservative. He resigned the foreign
secretaryship in 1878 and two years later joined the
Liberals. Disraeli appears never to have made any public
declaration of the undesirability of 'entangling alliances',
and his correspondence as Prime Minister with Queen
Victoria, with Northcote and with Salisbury reveals no
aversion as a matter of general principle from continental
involvements. Salisbury during his second and third
administrations repeatedly explained the impossibility, and
less frequently the undesirability, of giving any pledge
binding Britain's future action, but his public statements
on this subject were not numerous.[16] Indeed, public
declarations by leading Conservatives of the advantages
of freedom from alliances with other powers were not
common in the closing years of the nineteenth century.
The most striking was probably that by Goschen at
Lewes on 26 February 1896. Goschen, however, had
joined the Conservative Party only comparatively
recently.[17] Lord Randolph Churchill, after his resignation
from Salisbury's second government, had preached the
need for a policy of almost complete non-intervention in
the affairs of the Continent,[18] but his lasting influence on
the party was slight. As for the press, it presents no simple
pattern. From time to time, however, certain Conservative newspapers and individual journalists with Conservative sympathies displayed some restlessness with the
existing state of affairs.[19] On the whole, devotion to the
'traditional policy', although it existed, seems to have
been considerably less strong among Conservatives than
among their Liberal opponents. In this respect, as in
some others, Salisbury was not altogether representative
of the party of which he was the leader.

The Liberal–Unionists present an interesting problem. During the general election campaign of 1880 Hartington had told a meeting at Rawtenstall, in the Lancashire constituency where he was a candidate, that Britain could best serve the cause of peace in Europe by 'having her hands free, and by not being entangled or hampered by any separate or special alliance with any Powers'.[20] In 1887 Chamberlain had been regarded by Dilke, who was in a good position to judge, as a politician who was particularly opposed to continental involvements.[21]

Nevertheless, within a few months of the formation of Salisbury's third government there was a rumour that the Liberal–Unionists, and more especially Chamberlain, wanted to jettison the 'traditional policy of freedom from all entanglements'.[22] Moreover, it is a curious fact that the members of Salisbury's Cabinet who showed themselves to be most in favour of a 'new departure' were all Liberal–Unionists. The story of Chamberlain's activities is well known. It was the Hanoverian-born wife of the Duke of Devonshire (as Hartington had now become) who arranged the meeting between Chamberlain and Eckardstein at Chatsworth in January 1901, and, if we may believe Eckardstein, the Duke participated in their discussion.[23] It was Lansdowne, who had been a junior member of Gladstone's first and, for a few months, of his second administration, who was the architect of the alliance with Japan, the case for which was also strongly urged at Cabinet level by Selborne, the First Lord of the Admiralty, another Liberal–Unionist and the son of a former Liberal Lord Chancellor.[24] Perhaps all this is no more than coincidence. It would certainly not be easy to prove that the Liberal–Unionists worked together as a group during Salisbury's last administration to bring about the overthrow of the 'traditional policy'.

At all events, whatever their party affiliations and whether they spoke of Britain's policy of 'isolation' or employed some other turn of phrase, a great many people in the later years of the nineteenth century and at the beginning of the twentieth were agreed on certain points: Firstly, that Britain was free from any alliance in the sense of a formal written agreement pledging her, should a certain stated contingency arise, to go to war in support of another power; indeed, this freedom was sometimes stated in terms so comprehensive as to imply, not merely that Britain was not bound by any alliance, thus defined, but that she was under no treaty obligation of any kind that entailed the *casus belli*. Secondly, that this freedom was deliberate — a matter of policy. Thirdly, that it was of considerable standing — in short, 'traditional'. These opinions were not universal, but they were certainly very common. They were, moreover, shared by both the defenders and the critics of the 'traditional policy' and by many observers outside Britain.

6 Legend or Reality?

IN recent years the notion of a deliberate attitude or policy of 'isolation' on the part of successive British governments in the later nineteenth century and at the beginning of the twentieth has, as already mentioned, come in for some severe criticism. One historian has referred to 'the legend of a policy of isolation'.[1] The validity of this view depends, of course, on what one understands by the term 'isolation'. Even when 'deliberately chosen', 'isolation' could mean more than one thing.

The term was sometimes employed in a sense so broad as to render it indistinguishable from the policy of 'non-intervention', of which Richard Cobden had formerly been the champion.

Thus, in February 1887 Salisbury wrote to Queen Victoria apropos of the German and Austro-Hungarian ambassadors: 'Hatzfeldt says that Karolyi [*sic*] always maintains that England will observe an attitude of absolute isolation — and he justifies that course by the familiar arguments of Mr Cobden.'[2] In 1896 Rosebery interpreted Goschen's reference in his Lewes speech to Britain's deliberately chosen 'isolation' as a 'boast that we were alone in Europe, and that under no circumstances would we have anything to do with any other nations'.[3] In his 'long spoon' speech on 13 May 1898 Chamberlain declared that for nearly fifty years 'the policy of this country has been a policy of strict isolation. We have had no allies — I am afraid we have had no friends'.[4] Clearly at no time in the later nineteenth century did Britain pursue a policy or adopt an attitude of 'isolation' in the broad sense of that term implied by these remarks and others that one could quote.

It is of course true that there were several occasions on which British governments, for one reason or another, declined to collaborate with other powers. In May 1876 Disraeli and Derby refused to adhere to the Berlin Memorandum, which embodied the proposals of Austria–Hungary, Germany and Russia for an armistice and reforms in Bosnia and Herzegovina, where a revolt against the Ottoman Empire had broken out the previous year. In April 1895 Rosebery and Kimberley decided not to join Russia, France and Germany in intervening in the Far East to demand the abrogation by Japan of the Treaty of Shimonoseki. All powers, however, decline on certain occasions to collaborate with others in intervening at particular junctures, if their interests so require. One could not build a theory of a sustained policy or attitude of 'isolation' on such episodes.

As a matter of fact, the intervention of Russia, France and Germany in the Far East was the occasion for a statement by Rosebery, in a letter to Kimberley, of the general principles which should guide any British government in deciding whether it should or should not intervene in any dispute. After examining the considerations that had led Britain, on the one hand, to take steps to protect Shanghai in the recent war and, on the other hand, to refrain from joining the three powers in action against the Treaty of Shimonoseki, Rosebery argued:

But the guiding principle in both cases is the same: we cannot embroil ourselves in the quarrels of others unless our own interests imperatively demand it. Imperatively, I say, because our commerce is so universal and so penetrating that scarcely any question can arise in any part of the world without involving British interests. This consideration instead of widening rather circumscribes the field of our action. For did we not strictly limit the principle of intervention we should always be simultaneously engaged in some forty wars.[5]

This is certainly a strong argument in favour of limiting British intervention to questions in which only her really vital interests were involved, but it is not a statement of a policy of 'isolation'.

In fact, particularly during Salisbury's second (1886–92) and third (1895–1902) administrations, Britain on several occasions collaborated with one or more of the great European powers. In 1887, for example, Salisbury went a considerable way in the direction of what he called 'relations plus intimes' with continental powers, when he negotiated the exchanges of notes known as the Mediterranean agreements, the first of which, that with Italy, he described to Queen Victoria on 10 February of that year as 'as close an alliance as the Parliamentary character of our institutions will permit'.[6] On the other hand, in September 1892, after the Liberals had returned to office, Rosebery, according to his own account, told Hatzfeldt that 'Lord Salisbury appeared to have entered into closer relations with Italy than I had felt myself justified in doing. . . . I did not think that I could persuade my colleagues to give any such note'.[7] Rosebery's attitude to the Mediterranean agreements was to take no cognizance of them.[8] In December 1892 Gladstone, according to Waddington, the French ambassador, who paid him a visit at Hawarden, denied the very existence of any written engagement with Italy — no doubt in good faith.[9]

Early in 1896 Salisbury reported to Monson, the ambassador in Vienna, that he had told the Austro-Hungarian ambassador that he was quite willing to renew the 'common declaration of Mediterranean policy' made by Britain and Italy in 1887,[10] and shortly afterwards he wrote to Lascelles in Berlin: 'We certainly wish to be good friends with Germany: as good friends as we were in 1892. That is to say, we wish to lean to the Triple Alliance without belonging to it.'[11] On 30 August 1898 Balfour, who was temporarily in charge of the Foreign Office during Salisbury's absence, signed with Hatzfeldt a convention relating to Portugal's overseas possessions, under which Britain and Germany secretly agreed, amongst other matters, to oppose the intervention of any third power in Mozambique, Angola and in Portuguese Timor.[12] On 15 October 1900 Salisbury and Hatzfeldt signed an agreement for the maintenance of the 'open door' in China.[13] During his third administration Salisbury also upheld the principle of the 'concert of Europe', and attempted, with varying success, to collaborate with other powers in solving the Armenian and Cretan questions and in the relief of the Peking legations.

As has been seen, however, an attitude or policy of 'isolation' could also be understood in a narrower sense, namely, the avoidance, at least in peace-time and when there was no immediate danger of war, of any formal alliance, entailing the *casus belli*. It has also been seen that in the last years of the nineteenth century and at the beginning of the twentieth it was believed by a great many people, including some who did not favour the term 'isolation' as a description of Britain's attitude towards other powers, that the avoidance of any such alliance was an established principle of British foreign

policy. It would have been strange if a belief so widely
held had been entirely without foundation.

Indeed, when in May 1898 her alleged policy of 'isolation' became the subject of controversy, it was, as a
matter of fact, almost exactly twenty years since Britain
had been a party to any treaty or convention that contained a formal pledge to resort to the use of force should
the *casus foederis* arise. The last such occasion had been on
4 June 1878, when Layard, the ambassador in Con-
stantinople, had, on instructions from Salisbury, signed
with the Porte the Convention of Defensive Alliance,
better known, from its most famous article, as the Cyprus
Convention. Moreover, the military undertaking given
on that occasion had been unilateral, had been limited to
the Asian territories of the Ottoman Empire, and had
been conditional on the implementation by the Porte of a
programme of reforms in the areas concerned.

No British government had committed the country to
go to war on any part of the continent of Europe since
August 1870, when after the outbreak of the Franco-
German War and the publication in *The Times* of the
Benedetti 'draft treaty', of 1866, which had caused concern in London for the future of Belgium, Granville had
negotiated treaties with both the North German Con-
federation and France for the protection of the independence and neutrality of that country. The obligations
incurred under these two treaties had been strictly
limited, in time to the duration of the war then in progress
and the ensuing twelve months, and in space to the actual
territory of Belgium.

Britain had not given a guarantee, in the strict sense of
that term,[14] of the territory or neutrality of any state since
11 May 1867, when she had been a party to the treaty,

E

signed in London, that had settled the Luxemburg problem. Stanley, the Foreign Secretary, who had represented Britain at the conference on Luxemburg, had not wished to include any guarantee at all in the treaty and had agreed to do so only under pressure.[15] The guarantee of Luxemburg was, in any case, only a 'collective' one, which was forthwith explained away in the House of Lords by the Prime Minister, the fourteenth Earl of Derby,[16] whose interpretation his son subsequently endorsed both in the House of Commons and in an interview with Bernstorff, the Prussian minister in London.[17] The stringency of the obligation entailed by the guarantee of Luxemburg, as explained by Derby and Stanley, was dismissed by Granville four years later as 'of an infinitesimal character'.[18]

On 13 July 1863 Britain had been a party to a treaty, also signed in London, providing for the accession of a Danish prince to the vacant throne of Greece. This treaty stated that Greece was under the guarantee of three of the signatories, Britain, France and Russia, but this guarantee itself rested on an earlier treaty, signed on 7 May 1832. (To be strictly accurate, the scope of the guarantee mentioned in the 1832 treaty was extended in 1863 to cover Greece's status as a constitutional and not merely as a monarchical and independent state.)

On 19 August 1858 Britain had been a party to a convention, signed in Paris, regulating the status of the recently united Principalities of Moldavia and Wallachia, which were to enjoy their privileges and immunities under the guarantee of all the signatory powers. This guarantee, however, also rested on a previous treaty, namely that of Paris, Article XXII of which had provided for the guarantee of the privileges and immunities of the as yet still separated Principalities. The 1858 convention merely applied this guarantee to the now united Principalities, at the same time qualifying it as 'collective'.

Britain had not given a specifically 'several' guarantee since 15 April 1856, when, together with Austria and France, she had been a party to the Tripartite Treaty, signed shortly after the conclusion of the Treaty of Paris, which had brought the Crimean War to an end. The Tripartite Treaty, which had declared that any infraction of the stipulations of the Treaty of Paris would be *casus belli*, and which Palmerston had described in the House of Commons as 'the triple alliance of England, France and Austria',[19] had, in fact, been the last treaty signed by Britain that had pledged her unequivocally and in circumstances that were not merely temporary to go to war on the continent of Europe, should the *casus foederis* arise.

The Tripartite Treaty was, however, a product of the situation created by the Crimean War, the preservation of the fruits of which it was expressly designed to ensure. It belonged, indeed, to an altogether earlier era in the history of British foreign policy — the Palmerstonian era — when Britain had undertaken a considerable number of treaty obligations entailing the *casus belli*. In the changed circumstances of the post-Palmerstonian period it would scarcely have been possible for a British government to undertake any such commitment. 'What sticks in my gizzard', wrote Granville to Gladstone on 10 December 1870, after Russia's repudiation of the Black Sea articles of the Treaty of Paris, 'is the Tripartite Treaty. How very foolish it was of us to have concocted it.'[20] As a matter of fact, the Tripartite Treaty had ceased to correspond with the realities of the international situation long before 1870, and when, in April 1877, Russia had invaded

Turkey, it had not been invoked by any of its signatories.[21]
The Porte, not being a signatory, was not entitled to
invoke it, as Derby, the Foreign Secretary, had been careful to explain in the House of Lords with evident satis-
faction.[22]

Thus in 1898 Britain, although not free from any pledge
to go to war *in casu foederis*, was at least free from any
recent pledge of that kind. More especially was she free
from any alliance with another great power comparable
with the Austro-German, the Triple or the Franco-
Russian Alliance. Her freedom of action, although less
than that of, for example, the United States, was, nevertheless, far greater than that enjoyed by any of the leading
powers of the Continent.

Moreover, although this was, of course, not known to
the public at large, Britain's freedom from any recent
treaty obligations entailing the *casus belli* was not the
result merely of reluctance on the part of other great
powers to seek her partnership. Since 1887 Salisbury had
received and politely declined repeated invitations to
conclude what Liberals would no doubt have called 'entangling alliances'. Thus, when in 1898 Joseph Chamberlain gave warning of the consequences of a continued
policy of 'isolation' there were, in fact, good grounds for
believing, as many people did believe, that the avoidance
of any alliance, in the sense of a formal written pledge to
go to war in a given contingency, was an established
principle of British foreign policy. Nevertheless, in the
following year, under pressure from events in Africa,
Britain gave just such a pledge.

The deterioration of Britain's relations with the South
African Republic in the eighteen-nineties had lent added
strategic importance to the port of Lourenço Marques on

LEGEND OR REALITY?   49

Delagoa Bay in the Portuguese territory of Mozambique, which constituted the Transvaal Boers' only point of access to the sea, other than through British territory. In 1875 a treaty between the then still fully independent South African Republic and Portugal had provided for the construction of a railway, and since 1895 Johannesburg and Pretoria had been linked with Lourenço Marques by rail. It was, therefore, essential for Britain to ensure that, in the event of war, Kruger's government should not be able to use Lourenço Marques for the import of armaments.

On 8 October 1899, the eve of the outbreak of war in South Africa, Salisbury wrote a private letter to Soveral, the Portuguese minister in London, inviting him to read Article I of the Anglo-Portuguese treaty of 1642, under which, he claimed, 'Portugal engages not "to adhere" to any Treaty hostile to Great Britain'. He referred to a French ship, which, he declared, was approaching Delagoa Bay with a cargo of 'mitrailleuses and other munitions of war for the Transvaal', and which, he complained, the Portuguese authorities declined to detain because of the twenty-four-year-old treaty between Portugal and the Transvaal. 'You say', wrote Salisbury, 'that you cannot stop it by reason of the Portuguese–Transvaal Treaty of 1875. But in "adhering" to that Treaty you are "adhering" to a Treaty hostile to Great Britain.'[23] Six days later, on 14 October 1899, after the Boer invasion of the British colonies in South Africa, Salisbury and Soveral signed a joint declaration, reaffirming all the 'ancient treaties' and more particularly Article I of the treaty of 1642, which Salisbury had just invoked, and the final article of that of 1661, under which Britain was pledged 'to defend and protect all conquests or colonies belonging to the Crown of Portugal'.[24] In fact, Portugal did not proclaim her neutrality in regard to the South African War, and the Boer Republics were thus deprived of what would otherwise have been their right as belligerents to import munitions through Lourenço Marques.

Of course, the Anglo-Portuguese declaration of 14 October 1899 was no more than a reaffirmation of existing treaties, the continued validity of which Salisbury had, in any case, recognized, only the previous year.[25] Moreover, Portugal was not a great power. The declaration clearly did not tie Britain's hands in the way that her adherence to the Triple Alliance would have done. In addition, the declaration was a highly secret one. Indeed, its history raises the question as to whether the popular beliefs concerning Britain's international position that were so frequently expressed at this period were or were not the result of imperfect information on the part of politicians and journalists, who were not acquainted with what went on inside the Foreign Office.

The fact is that the Anglo-Portuguese declaration of 14 October 1899 was not the only agreement concluded during Salisbury's second and third administrations that was not laid before Parliament. It had also been intended to keep the Mediterranean agreements of 1887 secret, but in this case there had been a leakage and rumours had circulated which exaggerated the significance of the undertaking given. In the House of Commons Labouchere had asked awkward questions and eventually, on 22 February 1888, had initiated a debate.[26] By the mid-nineties the fact that Salisbury had given some sort of undertaking to Italy and Austria–Hungary was widely recognized, although the details were, of course, not

known. Thus in 1896 Spenser Wilkinson wrote in *The
Nation's Awakening*: 'There is evidence tending to show
that during Lord Salisbury's last administration some
assurances . . . were given by him both to Austria and to
Italy.' On the other hand Wilkinson doubted whether the
assurances given by Salisbury still held good, especially in
view of the complacent references to Britain's 'isolation'
made recently, especially by Goschen. 'More than one
Cabinet Minister', he wrote, 'has quite recently referred to
the isolation of England in terms which are hardly con-
sistent with the existence of pledges of any kind to any of
the Great Powers.'[27]

Some two years later, on 25 April 1898, after one of his
conversations with Hatzfeldt, Joseph Chamberlain recorded that the German ambassador had that day referred
to 'conversations which he had had with Lord Salisbury
during the time of the last Conservative Government, in
the course of which he said progress had been made
towards an alliance with Italy and Austria', adding: 'I said
that I had no knowledge of these conversations.'[28]
No doubt Chamberlain's profession of ignorance was
strictly accurate, but he could scarcely have forgotten
Labouchere's persistent questions in the House and the
debate of a decade previously. The memorandum in
which Chamberlain recorded this interview was, however, intended for Salisbury, and it may well be that he
thought it tactful not to display knowledge of the inner
history of an administration of which he had not been a
member.

The Anglo-German convention of 30 August 1898 was
also intended to be secret. It was soon realized in London,
however, that Hatzfeldt's frequent visits to the Foreign
Office were significant, and early in September 1898 the

Pall Mall Gazette published an inaccurate account of what had been agreed, which, it claimed, amounted to an offensive and defensive alliance in certain circumstances, commenting, with reference to the principle that was supposed to have been abandoned: ' "Splendid isolation" is a magnificent phrase, but it is not diplomatic business.'[29] This was followed by the appearance of guarded statements in German newspapers, including the *Kölnische Zeitung* and the official *Norddeutsche Zeitung*, which gave a more accurate but not a detailed account of the nature of the convention. Within a few months the fact that the convention related to the Portuguese possessions in southern Africa and more particularly to Delagoa Bay become widely known.[30]

On the other hand, the secret of the Anglo-Portuguese declaration of 14 October 1899 appears to have been much better kept. Not merely was the declaration not laid before Parliament. Its text was not, according to Sir Thomas Sanderson, the permanent under-secretary at the Foreign Office, communicated even to the British minister in Lisbon.[31] Indeed, it is possible that it was not submitted to the Cabinet, although on this point it is difficult to speak with certainty. Negatives are hard to prove. Salisbury, who in 1899 was still both Prime Minister and Foreign Secretary, would have had no difficulty in withholding knowledge of the declaration from the Cabinet, if he had so desired. At all events, the public at large knew nothing, so far as can be judged, of what Salisbury had agreed with Soveral. One can therefore only speculate as to whether the supporters of the so-called policy of 'isolation' would have considered the Anglo-Portuguese declaration a violation of their principles, had they been aware of its existence.

7 'A Piece of Paper'

ALTHOUGH at the end of the nineteenth century Britain was free, apart from her commitment to Portugal, from any recently contracted obligation entailing the *casus belli*, it is, nevertheless, undeniable that much that was said at the time concerning her 'isolation', or, for that matter, her 'free hand' or her 'freedom from all entanglements', took little or no account of the existence of treaties and — to be strictly accurate — conventions, which, although concluded many years previously, had never been abrogated and were in theory, and, in some instances, in more than theory, still valid.[1] It was only possible for Goschen, for example, to declare, as he did on 26 February 1896, that 'our isolation' meant 'the freedom to act as we choose in any circumstances that may arise',[2] by closing his eyes to obligations that did, at least on paper, still limit that freedom.

Nor was this attitude a new one. During the later eighteen-sixties and the early eighteen-seventies Stanley,[3] Clarendon[4] and above all Gladstone had refrained from emphasizing the binding character of Britain's treaty obligations, which, they insisted, the government of the day must have the right to interpret in the light of whatever might be the circumstances, when and if the contingency envisaged in any particular treaty should happen to arise. 'I am not able to subscribe to the doctrine,' Gladstone told the House of Commons on 10 August 1870, after the events of that summer had raised

the question of the validity of the guarantee of Belgium,
'. . . that the simple fact of the existence of a guarantee is
binding on every party to it irrespectively altogether of
the particular position in which it may find itself at the
time when the occasion for acting on the guarantee
arises'.[5]

In 1871 this latitudinarian attitude had been challenged
by Salisbury. In March of that year he gave notice in the
House of Lords of a motion calling attention to the
numerous 'guarantees' — a term within which he at that
time, in common with many of his contemporaries, included all treaty obligations that entailed the *casus belli* —
that Britain had undertaken at various times and were still
binding upon her, and also to the paucity of the military
resources available to her for honouring them. Granville,
the Foreign Secretary, was not a little perturbed. 'Lord
Salisbury', he wrote to Queen Victoria, 'has given notice
of a question about the guarantees and international
obligations of Great Britain. Lord Granville cannot
imagine what public object he can have in moving such a
delicate question at this moment.'[6]

On 6 March 1871 Salisbury duly introduced his motion
— it was not, in fact, a 'question' — in the House of
Lords, stating the doctrine of the obligations incumbent
on a guarantor in terms that could hardly have been more
categorical.[7] His speech was, in fact, reminiscent of, and
may perhaps have owed something to, a dispatch on the
subject written by Canning in 1823.[8] He also requested
that a 'blue-book', containing a return of the texts of all
Britain's 'treaties of guarantee', which had been laid
before Parliament in 1859,[9] as a result, in all probability,
of the anxiety of the Conservative government, which had
been briefly in office at the time of the outbreak of the

Franco-Austrian war of that year,[10] to demonstrate
Britain's freedom from any secret commitments, be
reprinted with the addition of all similar treaties concluded
since that date. Salisbury was answered by Granville, who
was at pains to avoid any precise statement concerning
the validity of the various treaties concerned and, where
possible, to emphasize their antiquity. 'No doubt', he
observed, 'these treaties exist, one of the most stringent
being the Treaty entered into four hundred years ago
with Portugal.'[11]

The 'blue-book' requested by Salisbury was duly laid
before Parliament three months later,[12] and was the
occasion, on 12 April of the following year, of a debate in
the House of Commons, when the Radical, Sir Wilfrid
Lawson, moved the presentation of a humble address
praying the Queen to take the necessary steps to bring
about Britain's withdrawal from all treaties that bound
her to intervene by force of arms in the affairs of other
nations.[13] Lawson's motion was easily defeated in a not
very large House after a debate in which Gladstone so
convincingly explained away the significance of the
various treaties included in the return, that, of them all,
only one, the Tripartite Treaty of 15 April 1856, need be
considered 'stringent'.[14] 'The truth is,' remarked Gladstone, 'with regard to these guarantees, they depend for
their recognition and fulfilment very much on the
national opinion of the time.'[15]

It was also on this occasion that Gladstone propounded
a theory of the rights and duties involved in a guarantee,
which he attributed to Palmerston:

I have often heard Lord Palmerston give his opinion of guarantees
both in this House and elsewhere; and it was a familiar phrase of his,
which, I think, others must recollect as well as myself, that while a

guarantee gave a right of interference it did not constitute of itself an obligation to interfere. . . . I think there is very great force in Lord Palmerston's observation.[16]

In 1877, during the crisis that preceded the outbreak of the Russo-Turkish War and thereby raised the question of Britain's obligations under her treaties relating to the Ottoman Empire, Gladstone again put forward this view, once again attributing it to Palmerston.[17] He argued similarly in 1878, claiming, not merely that the doctrine was Palmerston's, but also one traditionally held by the Foreign Office. 'Under cover of a doctrine of that kind,' added Gladstone, 'there is room enough to avoid most serious inconveniences that might arise from these guarantees.'[18] Having regard to what is known of Palmerston it is difficult to believe that he ever expressed the opinion that Gladstone attributed to him.[19] Nor does this opinion appear to have been a traditional one at the Foreign Office. Indeed, it would be interesting to know the source of the doctrine repeatedly expounded by Gladstone. Perhaps it is to be found in a speech delivered in the House of Commons in 1867 by Stanley in connexion with the guarantee of Luxemburg, apropos of which he had declared: 'It would, no doubt, give a right to make war, but it would not necessarily impose the obligation.'[20] Stanley applied this argument, however, only to a 'collective' guarantee. It would seem that it was Gladstone who first extended Stanley's theory concerning 'collective' guarantees to guarantees in general. However, Gladstone's minimization of the duties of a guarantor aroused little protest at the time.

In the summer of 1898 Salisbury found himself in a position very similar to that in which he had placed Granville twenty-seven years previously. On 15 July 1898

a Liberal back-bench member of the House of Commons,
a certain Thomas Hedderwick, who no doubt suspected
that the Unionist government was not above secretly
bartering away the country's cherished freedom of action,
asked for a new return to be laid before Parliament
setting forth the provisions of all treaties and conventions, of which Britain was a signatory, that contained any
engagement, guarantee or other undertaking in regard to
the territory or government of any other power.[21]

The work required of the Foreign Office should not
have been overwhelming. All that was necessary was to
bring the 1871 'blue-book' up to date by the inclusion of
all treaties of the kind specified that had been concluded
since 1871 and the omission of any that had been abrogated since that date. Nevertheless, it was not until the
beginning of the following session, 7 February 1899, that
the return of 'treaties containing guarantees or engagements by Great Britain in regard to the territory or
government of other countries', asked for by Hedderwick, was laid before Parliament.[22] The nature of the
contents of this new 'blue-book' was, presumably, decided by Salisbury, as Foreign Secretary. At all events,
his hand is probably to be seen in the omission of the
Tripartite Treaty of 1856, which had been printed in the
'blue-books' of 1859 and 1871 and had never been
formally abrogated, but which Salisbury had for many
years regarded as the classic example of a treaty that was
stringent on paper, but totally ineffective in practice.[23]

Despite this significant omission, the array of theoretically valid treaties and conventions set forth by the
Foreign Office might at first sight be considered impres-
sive. Britain was shown to be pledged by a treaty signed
at Stockholm on 21 November 1855 with France and

Sweden — to be strictly accurate, the kingdom of
Sweden and Norway — to defend the latter's territory
against attack by Russia; by the Convention of Defensive
Alliance, better known as the Cyprus Convention, of
4 June 1878, with the Ottoman Empire, to defend the
latter's Asian territories, also against Russia; by a long
series of treaties going back to 1373 to defend Portugal;
and, by a treaty concluded in 1661, Portugal's overseas
possessions; all the 'ancient treaties' with Portugal had
been renewed in 1815.

The contents of the 1899 'blue-book' may also perhaps
have served as a reminder to those interested — who do
not appear to have been very numerous — that in the
years from 1815 to 1867 Britain, in common with other
great powers, had been a party to a considerable number
of treaties that contained articles providing for guarantees
of various matters, including possession of territory and
neutrality, and that, at least in theory, these, like all
guarantees, had no time-limit.

Thus, by Article XVII of the Treaty of Vienna of
9 June 1815 Britain had guaranteed Prussia's possession of
the territory that, by another article of the same treaty,
she had acquired from Saxony. By a treaty signed in Paris
on 20 November 1815 she had guaranteed the territorial
integrity and inviolability of neutral Switzerland; by one
signed in London on 7 May 1832 she had agreed that
Greece should form an independent and monarchical
state under her guarantee and that of France and Russia.
By the treaty of 19 April 1839, signed in London and
destined in the twentieth century to be rendered famous,
she had guaranteed no fewer than twenty-four articles
relating to the kingdom of Belgium, established after the
revolt of 1830, the seventh of which provided that

Belgium should form an independent and perpetually neutral state. By the Treaty of Paris of 30 March 1856 — to be carefully distinguished from the Tripartite Treaty — she had guaranteed, in common with the other leading powers, the independence and territorial integrity of the Ottoman Empire; guaranteed, without qualification, the free navigation of the Danube and the privileges and immunities of Moldavia and Wallachia; and guaranteed, collectively, the rights and immunities of Servia. She had been a party to the convention of 19 August 1858 concerning the United Principalities of Moldavia and Wallachia and to the treaty of 13 July 1863 concerning Greece, already mentioned. Finally, by a treaty signed in London on 11 May 1867 she had, collectively with the other great powers and with the Netherlands, guaranteed Luxemburg as a perpetually neutral state.

Of the treaties and conventions included in the 1899 return one, at least, might reasonably be regarded as defunct, namely that signed at Stockholm in 1855, although as late as 1905 Lansdowne still professed, perhaps not very seriously, to regard it as still in force.[24] France was now allied with Russia, the very power against which the treaty had originally been directed. Clearly by 1899 the Treaty of Stockholm had ceased to be anything more than an interesting historical survival.

The case of the Cyprus Convention of 4 June 1878 was more complicated. It had been negotiated by Salisbury himself at a period that was not so very remote. On the other hand, it had been most severely criticized in Britain, and its conclusion had soon been regretted by the Porte. Moreover, the reforms in the Ottoman Empire's Asian territories, which were the condition of the British military undertaking, had never materialized. On the

contrary, those territories had recently been the scene of
the notorious Armenian massacres. In 1896 Curzon, then
parliamentary under-secretary for foreign affairs, had
informed the House of Commons that, since the Ottoman
Empire had not fulfilled its side of the bargain, the corres-
ponding obligations on the British side had lapsed.[25] How
then was it that in 1899 the convention was still recognized by the Foreign Office as valid? Presumably the
explanation is that it constituted the sole contractual basis
of Britain's position as occupying power in Cyprus. As
long as the continuance of the occupation of that island
was held to be necessary the convention must be regarded
as being still in force.[26] But it is difficult to believe that in
1899 anyone in Britain took the obligations, as distinct
from the advantages, of the Cyprus Convention seriously.

There could, on the other hand, be no doubt as tot he
validity of Britain's alliance with Portugal, despite the
antiquity of the treaties on which it rested and the fact
that not all British Foreign Secretaries had been equally
categorical in their recognition of the obligations that
they entailed.

In 1852 Granville had asked Howden, the minister in
Madrid, not to allow the Spanish government to imagine
that Britain would for any reason withhold from Porgu-
gal 'that assistance, which she has a right by existing
treaties to claim'.[27] In 1873, when, during the period of
the short-lived first republic in Spain, there had been talk
of the possibility of intervention in Portugal by Spanish
republican elements, he had reminded the Spanish
minister in London of Britain's treaty obligations to
Portugal, to an attack on whose territory she could not be
indifferent.[28] When writing to Lisbon, however, he had
made it clear that the British government reserved the

right to judge for itself the circumstances in which it would respond to an appeal by Portugal.[29] In any case Granville said nothing about Portugal's overseas possessions. In 1876 Derby had briefly approved the assurance given by Lytton, the minister in Lisbon, of Britain's continued interest in the preservation of Portugal's independence.[30] In 1891, when Britain was involved in a dispute with Portugal over territory in south-eastern Africa, Salisbury had been extremely reserved. 'It is doubtful', he had written to Queen Victoria on 19 February of that year, 'how far under any circumstances Great Britain is bound *by treaty* to come to the succour of the King of Portugal if his independence is threatened.'[31]

During his third administration, however, Salisbury found it politic to uphold a stricter interpretation of the obligations entailed by the 'ancient treaties'. In 1898 there was talk of the possibility that Portugal, whose financial position was one of great embarrassment, might raise a foreign loan on the security of the customs revenue of one of her overseas possessions. On 22 June of that year Salisbury reported that Soveral, the Portuguese minister in London, had asked him what view the British government took of the 'ancient treaties'. 'I informed him', wrote Salisbury, 'that we quite recognized their present validity, allowing for such alterations as the lapse of time and change of circumstances would involve. We took up the same position with regard to them as that assumed by Lord Granville twenty-five years ago.'[32] In the following year Granville's dispatch of 19 February 1873, reporting the conversation in which he had explained his attitude, was printed in the new return of 'guarantees or engagements'.[33] On 8 October 1899 Salisbury, faced with the necessity of ensuring that the South African Republic

F

should not be able to import munitions through Lourenço Marques, invoked the Anglo-Portuguese treaty of 1642, thereby recognizing its validity. Six days later all the 'ancient treaties' were reaffirmed.[34]

The question of the interpretation of Britain's treaty obligations to Portugal arose once again in the closing months of Salisbury's premiership. On 5 March 1902 the Intelligence Division of the War Office submitted to the Foreign Office a memorandum, drawn up by a certain Lieutenant-Colonel Robertson (better known to history as Field-Marshal Sir William Robertson), on Britain's 'military responsibilities' with regard to a number of countries in northern and western Europe, accompanied by a request for guidance as to whether certain treaties with some of the countries concerned were regarded officially as still being in force, in order that their strategic implications might be studied and plans for appropriate action worked out.[35] Among the countries listed as one towards which Britain had treaty obligations was Portugal, under a treaty of 1703, which had been renewed in 1815. In due course this memorandum reached Lansdowne, who recognized the validity of the treaties of 1703 and 1815, subject, however, to an important qualification. 'We may reply to the questions asked of us,' he wrote on 17 March 1902, 'by saying that the Treaties mentioned are still in force, but that although we should certainly have to assist Portugal, we do not find in them any obligations which would render it incumbent upon us to do so by means of a landing in Portugal.'[36] Lansdowne, understandably, did not mention the Anglo-Portuguese declaration of 14 October 1899.

The 'ancient treaties' were, of course, the expression of an important British interest. 'If the independence of the

Sovereign of Portugal was threatened,' wrote Salisbury to Queen Victoria on 19 February 1891, 'it would probably be the *interest and policy* of Great Britain to assist her.'[37] In November 1899, after the Kaiser and Bülow had visited Windsor and seen Chamberlain, Francis Bertie wrote to Bigge, the Queen's private secretary: 'I can only hope that Mr C. has not given any encouragement to the idea of killing the goose. She [Portugal] does not lay golden eggs, but she would be of great use to us in the event of a war in which we had to operate in the Mediterranean and South Atlantic and we do not want her Islands to pass into other hands — than our own.'[38] 'It is ... to our interest', wrote Robertson in his memorandum on Britain's 'military responsibilities', 'that the Portuguese Colonies — especially Mozambique — should not fall into other hands.'[39] The 'ancient treaties' were also, owing to Portugal's geographical position and Britain's command of the sea, comparatively easy to honour. In discussions of Britain's 'isolation', however, little or nothing appears to have been said concerning these historic engagements.

Nor in the course of such discussions does much appear to have been said, so far, at least, as has been recorded, concerning Britain's obligations as a guarantor, as distinct from an ally. Although the guarantees embodied in the treaties set forth in the 1899 return were numerous, they had all been given a good many years previously and in circumstances very different from those of the eighteen-nineties. The most recent of them, that of Luxemburg, dated from 1867. The fact is that by the late nineteenth century a guarantee, in the strict sense of that term, whether of a state's possession of territory or of its neutrality, had come to be regarded as an unsatisfactory

and outmoded device.[40] It was an arrangement that
seemed to belong to the past. It is understandable, therefore, that little was heard of Britain's obligations under
the numerous guarantees, of which she had formerly been
so prodigal.

Even the treaty signed in London on 19 April 1839,
under which Britain, together with Austria, France,
Prussia and Russia, had guaranteed the independent and
perpetually neutral state of Belgium, seems to have occupied only a small place in the national consciousness.
At the time of the Franco-German War of 1870 Gladstone
and Granville had not considered the guarantee given by
the powers more than thirty years previously an adequate
safeguard of Belgian independence and neutrality. The
guarantee had not, contrary to what is sometimes stated,
been renewed, but it had been supplemented by *ad hoc*
treaties with a rigid time-limit, concluded by Granville on
9 and 11 August 1870 with the North German Confedera-
tion and with France. On 10 August Gladstone, speaking
in the House of Commons, had minimized the obligations
entailed by the 1839 or by any guarantee.[41] When, on 12
April 1872, the Commons had discussed Lawson's
motion, the guarantee embodied in the treaty of 1839 had
not been one that Gladstone had been prepared to
recognize as 'stringent'.[42]

At the beginning of 1887 Dilke, a well-informed ob-
server of international affairs, had raised the question of
what Britain's attitude should be, if the neutrality of
Belgium were to be violated in a future war between
France and Germany. In an anonymous article in the
Fortnightly Review for January 1887 he pointed out that
France's frontier with Germany was now so strongly
fortified that, were war to break out, Germany would in

all probability send troops through Belgium. 'Is it quite certain', asked Dilke, 'that in a duel between Germany and France any of the Powers would think of coming to the assistance of Belgium?' That Britain had treaty obligations towards Belgium would, he argued, hardly be a sufficient argument to induce Parliament to sanction single-handed intervention against the violator of her neutrality. As for the treaty of 1839, memories of it had, he thought, become 'dim'.[43] Dilke's article was also published, in an inaccurate French translation, in the January 1887 number of the *Nouvelle Revue*, in which his incontestable statement that 'the treaty [of 1839] is not in the most modern form'[44] was rendered as 'l'ancien traité est tombé en désuétude'.[45]

The Belgian government and press naturally showed concern, and Vivian, the British minister in Brussels, wrote back to Iddesleigh,[46] and then, after Iddesleigh's death, to Salisbury, explaining the Belgian attitude.[47] On 1 February 1887 he wrote privately to Salisbury, emphasizing the anxiety felt in Belgium regarding the danger to which the country would be exposed by a war between France and Germany, which was believed to be 'inevitable if not imminent'.[48] (Boulanger was in office in France at this time as Minister of War and approaching the height of his popularity.) On 4 February a letter written by Alfred Austin and published over the pseudonym of 'Diplomaticus' appeared in the *Standard*, arguing that if, in the event of a Franco-German war, Belgium were to be invaded, Britain 'could not take part with France against Germany'.[49] Other London papers took up the subject, minimizing or denying altogether the existence of Britain's treaty obligation to Belgium.[50]

On 5 February Vivian again wrote to Salisbury,

reporting that he had told the Belgian Foreign Minister, de Chimay, 'not to attach any importance to a Newspaper Article as it was a mistake to suppose that the "Standard" or any other Paper was the official or even inspired organ of Her Majesty's Government'.[51] A week later he wrote again to say that de Chimay had anxiously enquired whether the articles in the London press were to be considered as an indication of a change in British policy in regard to the support of Belgium's neutrality.[52] Salisbury was normally a conscientious correspondent, but on this occasion the guidance requested by Britain's representative in Brussels was not forthcoming.[35] The only dispatch that Salisbury appears to have written in connexion with this episode was one in which he approved the language used by Vivian on the subject of the *Standard*.[54] Eventually Vivian concluded from Salisbury's silence that the British government considered it 'inopportune or inexpedient to express any opinion on the validity of the Treaty Guarantee of the neutrality of Belgium or to commit themselves in any way as to their future policy'.[55]

That the maintenance of the neutrality and independence of Belgium was a vital British interest was, of course, an opinion that was widely, although not universally, held.[56] Considerations of interest and of obligation are, moreover, not always easy to distinguish. Nevertheless, when examining the views expressed, not only during Salisbury's last administration, but for a good many years previously, concerning the British attitude to a hypothetical invasion of Belgium, it is impossible not to be struck by the slightness of the importance apparently attached to the 1839 treaty, on which alone the guarantee of that country's neutrality rested. The treaty was, for example, not so much as mentioned in the exchanges between the War Office and the Foreign Office in 1902.[57] It would be interesting to know whether anyone ever thought it worth while to point out that, if Britain really recognized the validity of this obligation, it was scarcely logical to talk of her policy of 'isolation'.

There seems to be little doubt that opinion in Britain concerning the sanctity of treaty obligations evolved considerably in the course of the later nineteenth century. Of this evolution there is no more striking example than that afforded by Salisbury himself. On 6 March 1871 he had upheld uncompromisingly the principle of the binding character of what was then generally termed a guarantee. His speech on that occasion was, in fact, an eloquent defence of the sacred nature of treaty obligations in general. Almost exactly two decades later, on 29 July 1891, he spoke at the Mansion House in different vein:

I am quite sure that we exaggerate too much the importance and the effect of treaties. In this age of the world, and in view of the fearful risk which every disturbance of the peace brings upon any nation concerned in it, I do not think that we must rate too high the effect of the bonds constituted by signatures upon a piece of paper. If nations in a great crisis act rightly they will act so because they are in unison and in cordiality with each other, and not because they have bound themselves to each other by protocols.[58]

In the third week of March 1902 Robertson's memorandum on Britain's 'military responsibilities', minuted at some length by Lansdowne and Sanderson, reached Salisbury. He was unco-operative. 'It does not seem to me', he wrote, 'that much profit will be derived from meditations of this kind. At least, I am sure I can make no useful contribution.' Salisbury went on to argue that any attack on Belgium, Holland or Sweden would probably be preceded by some sympathizing movement from within, and he emphasized the difficulty of foreseeing the effect of such a movement on British opinion or the identity of the persons responsible for the conduct of British foreign policy, if the hypothetical situation should arise. 'Our treaty obligations', he added, 'will follow our national inclinations and will not precede them.'[59] These words read like an echo of those uttered by Gladstone in the House of Commons nearly thirty years previously in the course of the speech in which he had so persuasively explained away the treaty obligations to which Salisbury had himself drawn Parliament's attention.

8 Salisbury and 'Splendid Isolation'

To no statesman of the later Victorian era has a fondness for 'isolation' and more especially, of course, for 'splendid isolation', been so often attributed by historians as to Salisbury. Whereas Joseph Chamberlain is generally associated with the first attempt to end Britain's 'splendid isolation', Salisbury is commonly represented as its leading and most tenacious defender. 'Le vieux Salisbury', writes Professor Maurice Baumont, 'incarne avec un calme imperturbable le "splendide isolement".'[1] It would be easy to quote similar examples of what is clearly a widely held opinion.[2]

During his own lifetime Salisbury was seldom, if ever, singled out in this way, at any rate by his fellow-countrymen. German diplomats, on the other hand, were divided on the subject of Salisbury's views. In 1896 Hatzfeldt thought that he was in no way an adherent — 'durchaus kein Anhänger' — of 'splendid isolation'.[3] Five years later Holstein, who distrusted Salisbury, expressed a different opinion. The British Prime Minister, he wrote to Chirol, had 'in all probability determined to stick to isolation, and to await the great continental war, which he thinks must come some day'.[4] In Britain during the years 1895–1902 'isolation' was, of course, sometimes referred to as the policy of the government over which Salisbury presided. But it was also regarded as a 'traditional',[5] even a 'historic'[6] policy, which had been followed by successive governments, both Liberal and

Conservative, for many years past and which Salisbury had merely inherited and continued. More than once it was said to go back to the Crimean War. Salisbury was not associated in the public mind with any stirring declaration in favour of 'isolation', however 'splendid'. Still less was he regarded as the originator of the policy of 'isolation'.

It is significant that studies of Salisbury and of British foreign policy in general published during the two decades that followed his retirement do not attribute to him any fondness for 'splendid isolation' or, indeed, for 'isolation' of any kind. In fact, it seems that William Harbutt Dawson, who was, in all probability, the first historian to attribute, in 1923, to Britain an attitude of 'splendid isolation' was also the first to associate Salisbury with that attitude.

Dawson's comment on Salisbury's alleged 'preference for the old national attitude of "splendid isolation" '7 has had many echoes. Nevertheless, its validity has not gone unchallenged. In the fourth volume of her biography of her father, published in 1932, Lady Gwendolen Cecil sharply criticized what she called 'the tradition which ascribes to him [Salisbury] an acquiescence, and even pride, in isolation', which, she maintained, 'is wholly negatived by his correspondence'. 'The theories', added Lady Gwendolen, 'as to his policy which have been built upon that oft-quoted phrase of "splendid isolation" are a warning as to the dangers of unverified quotation.'8 It would not be correct to say that this vigorous protest produced no effect whatever. Nevertheless, what Lady Gwendolen called the 'tradition' concerning Salisbury is still powerful.

There is certainly not a great deal in Salisbury's *ipsissima verba* on which to base the tradition concerning him. In the eighteen-sixties 'isolation' had been the consequence of the failure of successive British governments to follow the example set by Castlereagh;[9] in the eighties of the inept policy of Gladstone and Granville.[10] In 1877 Salisbury had warned Beaconsfield against a 'policy of isolation'.[11] A decade later 'isolation' was another and uncomplimentary name for the doctrine of 'non-intervention'.[12] The first Mediterranean agreement, which he concluded shortly after taking over the Foreign Office for the third time, was an insurance against what might ensue if, as he wrote to Queen Victoria, 'England was left out in isolation'.[13] A year later 'isolation' was something of which, as he again explained to the Queen, Britain, now stood in no 'special danger'.[14] In January 1896, after Hatzfeldt had dwelt on the subject, 'isolation' was less dangerous than 'being dragged into wars which do not concern us' — this also comes from a letter to the Queen.[15] In his 'dying nations' speech on 4 May 1898 'isolation' was something about which some person or persons unnamed talked 'jargon'.[16] On 29 May 1901, after Hatzfeldt had returned to his earlier theme, belief in the perils of 'isolation' lacked any historical justification.[17] It does appear ever to have been Salisbury's habit to describe his own foreign policy as one of 'isolation'.

As for 'splendid isolation', this phrase was not merely, contrary to what is sometimes stated, not coined by Salisbury; it was not even one of which he made frequent use. One occasion on which he did so was at the Lord Mayor's Banquet at the Guildhall on 9 November 1898, but what he said that evening had little or nothing to do with any of the notions with which 'splendid isolation' was usually associated. Salisbury was referring to Britain's comfortable remoteness from the Ottoman Empire, at that time the scene of the Armenian massacres, and dissociating himself from criticisms of other powers for not displaying a 'philanthropic spirit', which in their geographical situation they could not afford.[18] Salisbury was, no doubt, in a genial post-prandial mood and probably enjoyed employing the catch-phrase that a few months previously had caught the popular fancy to convey a meaning very different from that usually intended by those whose taste in oratory was more flamboyant than his own.

Salisbury also made a bantering reference to Britain's 'splendid isolation' in an altogether different connexion in the course of a speech that he delivered in the House of Lords on 30 January 1900. On this occasion he was pointing out how Britain's arrangements for the conduct of war — a field in which she was at that time experiencing some difficulty — differed to her disadvantage from those of the great powers of the Continent. 'Do not understand for a moment', he explained, 'that I am guilty of such profanity as to blame the British constitution. I am not. I am pointing out that in this matter we enjoy splendid isolation.'[19] Salisbury was not, of course, discussing foreign policy. In fact, the first example of Britain's 'splendid isolation' that he cited was her lack of a system of conscription. For Salisbury, unlike Chamberlain and Goschen, 'splendid isolation' was not a concept to be taken very seriously.

Dawson's attribution to Salisbury of a preference for 'splendid isolation' was not, of course, intended to be disparaging. In fact, it was made in the course of a eulogistic appreciation of Salisbury's work as Foreign Secretary. Nevertheless, it describes Salisbury's outlook in terms which that statesman would not, in all probability, have himself employed, at least in that connexion. A far more characteristic formulation of Salisbury's attitude towards the conduct of foreign policy is to be found in the speech that he delivered at Caernarvon on 10 April 1888:

We belong to a great community of nations, and we have no right to shrink from the duties which the interests of the community impose upon us. There is all the difference in the world between good-natured, good-humoured effort to keep well with your neighbours, and that spirit of haughty and sullen isolation which has been dignified by the name of 'non-intervention'. We are part of the community of Europe, and we must do our duty as such.[20]

This edifying pronouncement should not, of course, be thought of as providing an infallible key to Salisbury's diplomacy. But it is certainly more typical of his serious pronouncements on foreign affairs than the words applied to him by Dawson and so often repeated.

Dawson's comment on Salisbury is also in marked contrast to the opinions concerning him expressed by several persons well qualified to judge. In October 1902, for example, shortly after Salisbury's retirement, an anonymous but well-informed contributor to the *Quarterly Review* described his conduct of foreign policy as a compromise between 'the old principle of avoiding entangling alliances . . . and the then prevailing tendency to great alliances, judiciously adjusted to a highly complex international situation'.[21] In the following year, after Salisbury's death, Wilfrid Scawen Blunt recorded the opinion that he had 're-established in large measure England's influence on the Continent'[22] Neither of these authors saw fit to attribute to Salisbury any preference for 'splendid isolation'. Nor is any such comment to be found in Rosebery's tribute to Salisbury, delivered at the Oxford Union in 1904,[23] or in the discerning memoir of him written by Hicks Beach — or, rather, Earl St Aldwyn, as he had now become — ten years later.[24]

9 Salisbury and the *casus belli*

ALTHOUGH it was never Salisbury's habit to describe his own foreign policy as one of 'isolation' and it is evident that he resented the application of that term to his own handling of foreign affairs, the responsibility for the maintenance of the attitude towards other powers that was so frequently, if imprecisely, described by many of his contemporaries as that of 'isolation', with or without the well-known epithet, must to some extent be his. After all, between 1878 and 1900 Salisbury was Foreign Secretary for four periods totalling altogether approximately thirteen and a half years. Between 1885 and 1902 he was Prime Minister for three periods also totalling approximately thirteen and a half years. No other person in the later nineteenth century controlled the conduct of British foreign policy so completely and for so many years. If Britain had a policy of 'isolation' at all — and Chamberlain, Dilke, Balfour and Lansdowne all claimed that she had, and Goschen and Harcourt used language that amounted to much the same thing — that policy must have been, at least in part, Salisbury's.

Moreover, it is a fact that during both his second and third administrations Salisbury did on a large number of occasions declare his inability and a good deal less frequently his unwillingness to give any pledge to another power that would entail any obligation to resort to the use of force in a given contingency. In practice this negative attitude did amount to very much the same thing as what many of Salisbury's contemporaries, less fastidious than he was in matters of diplomatic terminology, meant when they spoke or wrote of a policy of 'isolation'.

Salisbury justified these refusals on more than one ground. His favourite argument, however, was a constitutional one. Britain's popular and parliamentary institutions, he maintained, made it impossible for the British government to give any assurance, engagement, pledge or promise to go to war in the future and in a hypothetical contingency, since the ultimate decision on questions of peace or war must lie with Parliament, and it was impossible to foresee what Parliament's attitude would be, should the contingency provided against happen to arise, since that would depend on the circumstances of the case and on the state of public opinion at the time. There could, therefore, be no certainty that any treaty or other agreement entailing the *casus belli* would be honoured, should it at any time be invoked.

Salisbury did not, of course, invent this constitutional argument. One very similar to it appears in a dispatch written on 25 June 1867 by Stanley, as he then was, in connexion with the guarantee of Luxemburg, under the treaty signed in London some six weeks previously:

In a country like ours, no absolutely valid engagement could be entered into as to the course to be adopted at a future period, and under circumstances not now foreseen.

Questions of war or peace must be decided by the Parliament of the day.[1]

The belief that Britain's parliamentary constitution, with the frequent and unforeseeable changes of ministry and of policy that it entailed, rendered any reliable alliance with her impossible was also widespread on the Continent and especially in Germany,[2] where it went back to a much earlier period.³ Nevertheless, the repeated insistence on the principle that any engagement involving the *casus belli* was incompatible with the British constitution was especially characteristic of Salisbury.

Thus, on 18 August 1892, a few days after tendering the resignation of his second government, Salisbury wrote an important letter, addressed to Currie, the then permanent under-secretary at the Foreign Office, but really intended for Rosebery, his successor as Foreign Secretary. After explaining the significance of Britain's relations with Italy and through Italy with the other powers of the Triple Alliance, he added:

We have always refused to give any assurance of material assistance. I have said that no English minister could do so, because the action of an English ministry must depend on the national feeling at the moment, and the national feeling would be decided by the nature of the *casus belli*.'⁴

Again, on 4 February 1896, after a conversation with Deym, the Austro-Hungarian ambassador, he reported to the British ambassador in Vienna:

I told Count Deym to-day that in this country it was impossible to take any engagement involving an obligation to go to war; as the power of Her Majesty's Government to do so depended on the political sentiment prevailing at the moment when the necessity arose: and that sentiment it was impossible to foresee.⁵

Nearly a year later, on 20 January 1897, after a further disquisition to Deym on the working of the British constitution, he again reported to Vienna:

I said it was quite impossible for England to make any such engagement as that which he desired. The institutions under which we lived entirely prevented Her Majesty's Government from making any engagement with respect to the military or naval action of England upon contingencies which had not yet arisen. When these contingencies arose, they would be fully considered by the Parliament

G

and public opinion of this country, and no influence of any Government, and probably no promise into which any Government might have entered, would in such a case avail to prevent the country from acting upon its own views of what was right and expedient in such a matter.[6]

Salisbury's expositions of this argument were lucid, forceful and numerous. He elaborated it, with, of course, minor variations, in dispatches, in his private correspondence, in conversations with foreign ambassadors, on one occasion in the House of Lords,[7] and in a famous and oft-quoted memorandum, drawn up on 29 May 1901 after the Foreign Office had gone so far as to draft a project for a convention of defensive alliance with Germany.[8] Some of his pronouncements were directed more specifically against proposed secret agreements.[9] Most of them precluded any pledge, secret or public, that would constitute an attempt to tie the hands of any future government or Parliament on the fundamental question of peace or war.

What may be called Salisbury's constitutional principle was not, however, a matter of lifelong conviction. Salisbury appears to have adopted it comparatively late in his career. No expression of this principle is to be found, for example, in his article on 'The Foreign Policy of England', published in the *Quarterly Review* in 1864, or in his important speech on Britain's guarantee obligations and military resources, delivered in the House of Lords on 6 March 1871. Nor has an examination of his correspondence with Queen Victoria, with Beaconsfield and with Northcote in the period 1878–80 yield any indication that he upheld this principle during his first period at the Foreign Office.

It is, of course, true that on at least two occasions during Disraeli's second administration, in 1877, when he was still at the India Office, and in 1879 after Münster, the German ambassador, had paid a visit to the Prime Minister at Hughenden, Salisbury displayed a marked lack of enthusiasm for an alliance with Germany.[10] His comment on what appeared likely to be the collapse of the somewhat nebulous project of 1879 was: 'We are well out of it.'[11] Dislike of a particular proposal for an alliance should, however, be carefully distinguished from the view that all such involvements are incompatible with the constitution. In any case, in 1879 the strongest ministerial opposition to the suggestion of an alliance came not from Salisbury, but from Northcote.[12]

It is also true that at some time during the eighteen-seventies, probably after the outbreak of the Russo-Turkish War of 1877 and the passive attitude of the other powers principally concerned had underlined the ineffectiveness of the Tripartite Treaty of 1856, Salisbury came to the conclusion that the once common type of undertaking known as a guarantee was not a satisfactory method of protecting a weak state against attack by a stronger neighbour. Thus it was that the so-called Cyprus Convention, concluded with the Ottoman Empire on 4 June 1878, a few days before the opening of the Congress of Berlin, contained, contrary to what is sometimes stated, no guarantee article. It was, in the words of its preamble, a 'Convention of Defensive Alliance'. Moreover the omission of any provision for a guarantee from the convention was not the result of any oversight on the part of the Foreign Office. It was deliberate. Salisbury made this clear in the House of Lords on 29 July 1878:

Those misty and shadowy guarantees which bound you to everything in theory, and which turned out, in practice, to bind you to nothing, were anything but honourable to the character of European

diplomacy. . . . I think it is time that the practice of making pledges
of this kind was abandoned in the diplomacy of Europe. We claim,
at all events, that we have made a pledge which will be easily
understood by those whom it concerns.[13]

Salisbury's objection to 'misty and shadowy guarantees'
should, however, be distinguished from the principle
that he so often propounded in his later years. Although
the undertaking given to the Ottoman Empire in 1878
was, indeed, a conditional one, it clearly involved 'an
obligation to go to war', should the *casus foederis* arise.

The question therefore arises: When was it that Salisbury first adopted the view that there were insuperable
objections to any treaty or other agreement that entailed
the *casus belli*? To this question there can, in all probability, be no final answer. All that can be stated here is
that the earliest example of an expression by Salisbury of
a general objection to any such engagement that an
examination of much of his correspondence, of his
speeches and of reports of conversations with him sent
home by foreign ambassadors has revealed occurs in a
letter that he wrote to Queen Victoria on 2 February 1887.
In this letter, written a few days after he had for the third
time become Foreign Secretary, he described a conversation that he had had the previous day with Corti, the
Italian ambassador, to whom, he reported, he had explained that 'England never promised material assistance
in view of an uncertain war, of which the object and cause
were unknown'.[14] It was not long before Salisbury
elaborated this objection, emphasizing the constitutional
difficulty involved. An early example of his employment
of this constitutional argument is to be found in a
memorandum that he wrote for the Queen on 23 February
1887, after he had been made to feel, not for the last time,

that Hatzfeldt could be importunate in pressing for a declaration of what Britain's conduct would be in the event of a war on the Continent. 'No English Government', wrote Salisbury, 'can give definite military pledges of military or naval co-operation in a future contingency: because it cannot be sure that Parliament would make such a promise good.'[15]

What was the reason for Salisbury's adoption of this constitutional principle? Once again, this is a question to which there can be no certain answer. Salisbury was not given to analysing his own motives for the benefit either of his contemporaries or of posterity. Nevertheless, it is possible to suggest certain considerations, by one or all of which he may have been influenced.

First in order of time was probably the failure of the Cyprus Convention. No feature of the eastern settlement of 1878 was more bitterly criticized in Britain. From the moment of its publication the convention was assailed both by Derby, Salisbury's immediate predecessor at the Foreign Office, and by the Liberal Opposition. In the House of Lords on 18 July 1878 Derby declared:

Two years ago ... any man would have been thought insane who would have proposed what which has been now done; and when the bill comes in for payment, and the English people understand what they have bound themselves to, I am not at all sure that two years hence we may not find that public opinion on these questions is pretty much what it would have been two years ago.[16]

Gladstone also thought that 'insane' was not too strong a word in the circumstances. Three days later, in a speech at Southwark, he termed the convention 'an insane covenant'.[17]

In retrospect the Cyprus Convention can be seen to have been an unwise and ultimately unsuccessful attempt to fly in the face of the opinions of a large section of the nation. It proved, in fact, to be one of those unforeseen blessings that used formerly to descend from time to time upon the Liberal Party, providing its members with an issue on which all could unite in heartfelt indignation at the folly and iniquity of their Conservative opponents. Its history is also a striking illustration of the futility of undertaking any treaty obligation without being sure that it is acceptable to the party in opposition and will be honoured, if and when that party returns to office.

Another event that may well have influenced Salisbury's subsequent conduct and one the history of which is not wholly separable from that of the Cyprus Convention was the downfall of the Conservative Party at the general election of 1880, which has often been regarded as a hostile verdict on the foreign policy of the Beaconsfield administration, and, therefore, of Salisbury himself. It is not certain that this diagnosis is correct. What is important from the point of view of the development of Salisbury's ideas, however, is not so much the real cause of the Conservative defeat, but what Salisbury believed the cause of that defeat to have been. As a matter of fact, on 7 April 1880, when the outcome of the election was clear, Salisbury wrote Beaconsfield a letter that contained no reference to questions of foreign policy. 'The elections', wrote Salisbury, 'are a puzzle to me — and I have seen no cause which satisfactorily accounts for so sudden a change. I suppose bad harvests and bad trade have done the most.'[18] On the other hand, we have Lady Gwendolen Cecil's assurance that her father unhesitatingly accepted the verdict of the electorate as one primarily on the action of his own department.[19] Perhaps the truth is that, although he did not take this view at the time, Salisbury subsequently came to accept the popular explanation of the defeat of his party. If that were the case, it would help further to explain his reluctance during the later part of his career to make experiments in the field of foreign policy that might have disagreeable electoral repercussions. The Conservative Party could not afford another Midlothian.

During his second administration, formed after the home-rule crisis, Salisbury had additional reasons for caution. His government was dependent for its majority in the House of Commons on the support of the Liberal–Unionists, led by Hartington, whose belief in the desirability of maintaining Britain's 'free hand' was still, as far as one can judge, as strong as ever. After 1886 he also had to be careful not to leave any opening for attack by Churchill or to offend Goschen, who had replaced Churchill at the Exchequer.

The delicacy of Salisbury's position was fully appreciated by his old antagonist, Derby, who was now the leader of the small group of Liberal–Unionists in the House of Lords. On 3 January 1888 Waddington, the French ambassador, reported to the Quai d'Orsay, after a New Year's visit to Knowsley, Derby's country-house in Lancashire, where his host had expatiated on the political situation:

Aucun Cabinet anglais, m' a-t-il dit, ne prendra d'engagement avec les Puissances continentales; mon pays ne veut pas être pris dans l'engrenage d'une guerre politique ou d'équilibre européen; ... Lord Salisbury sait parfaitement que, s'il engageait l'Angleterre dans la Triple Alliance, il serait immédiatement renversé; la grande majorité des libéraux-unionistes est bien décidée à ne pas le suivre dans cette voie et, dans son propre parti, il y aurait bien des défections. S'il faisait appel au pays, vous verriez se renouveler ce qui s'est passé lorsque Lord Beaconsfield a été renversé, deux ans à peine après le Congrès de Berlin, où cependant il avait remporté un succès, tant les électeurs craignaient d'être entraînés par lui dans des complications continentales; or l'électorat d'aujourd' hui est encore plus résolument pacifique que celui de 1880. . . . Ajoutez à cela que Lord Randolph Churchill et ses amis sont dans le même ordre d'idées.[20]

A few weeks later Waddington reported observations by Granville to similar effect.[21]

It is not, of course, suggested that electoral considerations provide the sole explanation of Salisbury's unwillingness to give pledges to any of the powers of the Triple Alliance. Probably he would have declined to do so anyway. For one thing, there was no point in creating more difficulties with France. Nor do such considerations wholly explain Salisbury's adoption of and apparent devotion to his oft-expounded constitutional principle. Indeed, one is tempted to ask how seriously Salisbury took this principle. Was it really a matter of deep conviction? Or was it a dialectical device, which he found useful when confronted, as he so frequently was, with a request for a pledge of British armed support in some hypothetical contingency? Salisbury would not have been the first British Foreign Secretary to find it convenient to be able to refuse such a request on the ground of an alleged general principle. At any rate the objection to undertakings, especially secret ones, that entailed the *casus belli* vanished when, in October 1899, it was essential to deprive the South African Republic of imports of armaments.[22] Salisbury's constitutional principle was not, in fact, completely rigid. It admitted of an exception when British interests so required.

There seems to be no doubt that important changes in Salisbury's attitude towards foreign affairs took place in

the course of his career. The evolution — transformation
one should perhaps say — of his ideas concerning the
sanctity of treaty obligations, already mentioned, is a case
in point.[23] There was, indeed, a striking difference
between the Foreign Secretary of the Beaconsfield
administration — still a comparatively young man, im-
petuous, with limited sensitivity both to the feelings of
other individuals and to the convictions of a large section
of the nation, and liable to greet publicly the news of a
move on the diplomatic chess-board of the Continent in
language traditionally reserved for the announcement of
the Nativity[24] — and the cautious, reserved and experienced
diplomat and party-leader of the later years of the century.
Nor did this change in his outlook go unperceived by his
contemporaries. 'He is a very different Salisbury', wrote
Rosebery to Gladstone in 1891, 'to the Foreign Minister
of 1878 or the Prime Minister of 1885.'[25]

Rosebery's remark is also significant as an indication of
the attitude of Liberals towards Salisbury during the
later years of his career. He certainly came to enjoy
a considerable degree of respect from his political opponents, who recognized that in certain respects his ideas
and methods were nearer to their own than to those of
many members of his own party.[26] In January 1892 John
Morley visited Paris and saw Ribot, the French Foreign
Minister, who reported to Paul Cambon his opinion,
expressed apropos of the Egyptian question, that 'Lord
Salisbury . . . a des vues supérieures à celles de son parti'.[27]
This attitude on the part of Liberals became particularly
noticeable during Salisbury's third administration. Harcourt wrote to Morley: 'I believe Salisbury to be by
nature and conviction a man of peace.'[28] Algernon West
recorded in his diary that Morley had observed that

'Salisbury . . . is a very big man, who interested him as having a wider grasp of statesmanship than anyone else.'[29] There can be no doubt that Liberals greatly preferred his approach to foreign affairs to that of the Colonial Secretary. 'There is nothing', declared the *Daily News* on 1 December 1899 after Chamberlain's exposition at Leicester of the advantages of 'a new Triple Alliance', 'that makes us wish so much to hear Lord Salisbury as a speech on foreign politics from Mr Chamberlain.'[30]

A study of Salisbury's opinions would not, of course, be complete without an examination of his attitude towards one more engagement that undoubtedly entailed the *casus belli* and which, together with the Cyprus Convention of 4 June 1878 and the Anglo-Portuguese declaration of 14 October 1899, constitutes the third such engagement for which he was, in part at least, responsible. Salisbury was still Prime Minister when, on 30 January 1902, Lansdowne signed the agreement generally known as the Anglo-Japanese Alliance. This alliance, however, which Lansdowne himself described as 'an entirely new departure',[31] requires a chapter to itself.

WHEN, in November 1900, Lansdowne took over the Foreign Office from Salisbury, Britain's international position was still, in the popular view, one of 'splendid isolation'. Less than fifteen months later Britain had become the ally of Japan.

Until recently comparatively little was known about the negotiations that led up to the Anglo-Japanese alliance embodied in the agreement of 30 January 1902 — far less than about, for example, the abortive Anglo-German negotiations of the years 1898–1901. A fully documented account of the history of the Anglo-Japanese alliance has, however, been published recently by Dr Ian H. Nish.[1] It is not, therefore, proposed to describe in detail the negotiations that preceded the signature of the agreement. The chief purpose of this chapter is to discuss how far the alliance with Japan was regarded at the time, not merely as an important new step in British Far Eastern policy, but also as marking the abandonment of Britain's alleged policy of 'isolation', of which the adjective 'splendid' had by this time become a conventional embellishment.

It seems that the origins of the negotiations that led up to the agreement of 30 January 1902 are to be found in certain unofficial conversations that took place in London in July 1901 between Sir Claude MacDonald, the British ambassador in Tokyo, who had been recalled to the Foreign Office for consultation, and Hayashi, the Japanese ambassador. On 31 July 1901 Lansdowne himself saw

Hayashi and, according to his own report, drew attention to the similarity of British and Japanese interests and suggested a discussion with a view to the establishment of an 'understanding' between the two powers. On 14 August he again saw Hayashi and invited the Japanese government to put forward concrete proposals.

At the beginning of September 1901 the argument for a full-scale alliance with Japan was strengthened by a memorandum, drawn up by Selborne, the First Lord of the Admiralty. Britain's battleships in Chinese waters were, Selborne pointed out, greatly inferior in numbers to those of Russia and France combined. If Britain were to attempt to rectify this situation by adding battleships to those already on the China Station she would be left with no more than bare equality of strength in the English Channel and the Mediterranean, would strain her organization and incur extra expenditure. Some of the cruisers on the China Station were, in any case, already needed elsewhere. 'The case', wrote Selborne, 'would bear a different aspect were we assured of the alliance of Japan.' Together Britain and Japan would be able to outnumber France and Russia in Chinese waters both in battleships and in cruisers.[2] In other words, an alliance with Japan would serve the causes both of security and economy.[3]

On 16 October 1901 Hayashi again saw Lansdowne and submitted concrete proposals, on the basis of which the Foreign Secretary drew up a draft agreement. On 5 November he submitted his proposal for an agreement to the Cabinet, as Salisbury reported to King Edward VII:

In the first instance Lord Lansdowne brought before the Cabinet a projected agreement with Japan, which he has been negotiating since last June.[4] The object of it is that in any war between Japan and one other Power *we* should be neutral: and similarly if we were at war. If the war involved *two* Powers against Japan, we should thus be bound to join her: and similarly Japan would be bound to help us against any two Powers.

The decision of the large majority of the Cabinet was in favour of Lord Lansdowne's proposal.[5]

Thus the proposed agreement was approved in principle. As to his own opinion, Salisbury in his letter to the King revealed nothing.

Balfour was not in favour of what he called 'an offensive and defensive alliance with Japan', but on 5 November he arrived late and unbriefed for the meeting of the Cabinet, as he afterwards related:

No papers were circulated to me on this subject before the Cabinet: nor was there any warning that it was likely to be discussed. I was a few minutes late, and found the brief debate already in full swing — and the Cabinet not very anxious to hear any views on the general aspects of a problem, which they were treating in the main as one confined to the Far East. I ought perhaps to have insisted on pressing my views, but was taken so much by surprise that I should probably have done them very little justice.

It is understandable that in these circumstances Balfour found it difficult to put his case as forcefully as he would have wished, and that he was unable to prevent the Cabinet from taking a decision that he considered 'perhaps rather hasty'.[6]

Balfour, accordingly, did his best to make good his ineffectiveness at the Cabinet meeting by means of a memorandum, which he drew up on 12 December 1901 and addressed to Lansdowne. 'Hitherto,' he wrote, 'we have always fought shy of any such engagements, and, whether we have been right or wrong, we could at least say that we were carrying out a traditional policy of isolation which had proved successful in the past. We can say so no longer.' After referring to the unsuccessful negotiations for an alliance with Germany, which had taken place earlier in the year, Balfour then proceeded to show that he was an apt pupil of his uncle, whose favourite argument he accurately reproduced:

Hitherto, we have, as I understand it, rejected Germany's advances mainly for two reasons, (i) that a policy of alliances was contrary to the traditions of this country, and (ii) that it was scarcely possible for a Ministry to engage, that in certain contingencies, the country should go to war, since war was impossible without the support of Parliament, and, when the critical moment came, that support might be withheld. Neither of these arguments can any longer be employed. We have offered, in favour of Japan, to abandon our traditional policy, and we have proved in our own persons that a Ministry can promise to go to war in remote contingencies and over quarrels at present unforeseen.[7]

The British draft agreement, approved by the Cabinet on 5 November 1901, was presented to Hayashi, who a week later submitted a counter-draft. This, in its turn, was discussed and much criticized on points of detail by the Cabinet on 19 December. Lansdowne, accordingly, drew up a memorandum, dated 1 January 1902, explaining his proposal and the Japanese standpoint.[8] Several members of the Cabinet were critical and Salisbury set forth at length his views of the proposed agreement, as explained by Lansdowne. He took exception to Japan's refusal to extend the scope of the alliance beyond the Far East. He was even more disturbed at Lansdowne's admission that Japan would never accept any stipulation that would prevent her from taking without British consent measures that Britain might regard as provocative, but which she would consider forced upon her by the conduct of Russia.

But [added Salisbury], if that is their last word, the prospect held out by the Agreement in that form is somewhat disquieting. It involves a pledge on our part to defend Japanese action in Corea and in all China against France and Russia, no matter what the *casus belli* may be. There is no limit: and no escape. We are pledged to war, though the conduct of our ally may have been followed in spite of our strongest remonstrances, and may be avowedly regarded by us with clear disapprobation. I feel sure that such a pledge will not be sanctioned by Parliament, and I think in the interests of the Empire it ought not to be taken.[9]

Nevertheless, Salisbury did not reject the proposed alliance out of hand.

Despite these criticisms, the scope of the alliance, as finally agreed upon, was, in fact, limited to China and Korea. Britain and Japan, although disavowing any aggressive intentions, both recognized that it would be admissible for either of them to safeguard her interests in those countries, should they be threatened in any way. The *casus belli* would arise if either Britain or Japan were to find herself at war with a third power and a fourth power were to intervene on the opposing side, irrespectively of who had begun the original conflict.[10]

As for the reasons for Salisbury's acquiescence in these arrangements, which went beyond other proposals that he had previously rejected as incompatible with Britain's parliamentary institutions, one can only, once again, speculate. In the first place, as has been seen, Salisbury's objection to engagements involving the *casus belli* was, perhaps, not as absolute as at first might appear. In this connexion it is perhaps of some significance that in his memorandum of 7 January 1902 he did not employ his favourite constitutional argument to demolish Lansdowne's proposed agreement, as he had demolished the Foreign Office's draft treaty with Germany of the previous year. In any case he had already admitted in his letter to the King of 5 November 1901 that the proposal had the support of 'the large majority of the Cabinet'. Moreover, Salisbury, whose health had been failing for some time, was on the eve of retirement. He may well have felt that there was no point in resisting younger colleagues, who in a few months' time would be able to pursue whatever policies they pleased. Hicks Beach wrote later that, if Salisbury had still been Foreign Secretary at this period, the alliance with Japan would not have been concluded.[11]

On 30 January 1902 the Anglo-Japanese agreement was signed by Lansdowne and Hayashi, and a fortnight later it was published. The most obvious public reaction was one of surprise, particularly at the fact that the new alliance was not a merely defensive one. On 13 February Sir Edward Hamilton recorded in his diary what was probably a typical reaction:

An agreement signed and sealed with Japan — practically an offensive and defensive alliance — has transpired to-day and taken everybody by surprise. It is a very new departure. The avowed object of it is the maintenance of the *status quo* in China. The two Powers are to act together not merely when they are attacked, but when either of them is involved in war with more than one Power, owing to measures taken to defend its interests in China and Korea. On the whole, the Treaty seems to be well received.[12]

There were, in fact, differences of opinion as to the wisdom of the new move. Much, although by no means all, Liberal opinion was hostile, but there was no outcry comparable with that of 1878. Japan had not, after all, rendered herself obnoxious to a large section of the nation by any conduct comparable with that of the *bashi-bazouks* in Bulgaria in 1876. Moreover, she was regarded as having, by her recent exploits, particularly in connexion with the relief of the Peking legations in 1900, established herself as a modern power, worthy of partnership in an alliance of equals. To some people in Britain it evidently seemed that there were advantages to be gained from following the example of other powers and acquiring an ally. The new obligation, although not specifically limited to the use of naval forces, was clearly one in the discharge of which sea-power would play a decisive role. It was, moreover, a purely extra-European commitment.

There was, however, no disagreement whatever concerning the fact that Britain had given up what the *Spectator* called her 'fixed policy of not making alliances',[13] whether or not one chose to call that policy 'isolation' or to dignify it with the now well-worn epithet 'splendid'. 'The traditional policy of England in regard to alliances has been for half a century — ever since the ill-starred Crimean War — one of "splendid isolation",' wrote the *Daily News*, adding: 'Not only does it [the alliance with Japan] destroy at a blow our "splendid isolation"; it drags us into a union where all the essential advantages seem to be on one side.'[14] 'Our "isolation", splendid or otherwise,' observed the *Daily Chronicle* more dispassionately, 'is forsaken for a dual alliance.'[15] *The Times* described the alliance as 'a departure from the policy of isolation which England has so long pursued'.[16]

On 13 February 1902 the Anglo-Japanese agreement was debated in both Houses of Parliament. One Liberal after another emphasized the magnitude of the break with the past, which some, and especially Campbell-Bannerman and Harcourt, deplored.[17] Harcourt declared that the alliance meant 'the departure from principles which have been consecrated by the traditions of nearly a century'.[18]

H

The Unionists, although they defended the agreement, did not deny that Britain was abandoning her 'traditional policy'.[19] In the House of Lords Lansdowne observed that 'many of the arguments which a generation ago might have been adduced in favour of a policy of isolation have ceased to be entitled to the same consideration now'. He entreated his fellow-peers not to allow their 'judgment to be swayed by any musty formulas or old-fashioned superstitions as to the desirability of pursuing a policy of isolation'.[20]

The following day Rosebery, in a speech at Liverpool, commented ironically on what he called Lansdowne's 'recantation':

Yesterday in the House of Lords I was listening to the Secretary of State, not in a white sheet with a candle in his hand, but making with all the sound of triumph and congratulation a recitation and recantation of the once popular doctrine of splendid isolation. How much we heard of splendid isolation! How many tables were banged about splendid isolation! And now we come to the alliance with Japan. . . . The treaty with Japan may be our first treaty of the kind for many years, but, having made it, it cannot be the last.[21]

However, although he made fun of Lansdowne's abandonment of the 'once popular doctrine', Rosebery did not challenge the wisdom of the new move.

Lansdowne had, in fact, as Rosebery admitted, achieved what was widely regarded as a considerable diplomatic success, and for a few days was able to bask in the applause of his colleagues and of the public. On 16 February he wrote to thank Curzon, the Indian Viceroy, for his congratulations:

Your telegram as to the Japanese agreement pleased me much. It has been very well taken: better than I ventured to hope. I was prepared for a more widespread reluctance to abandon our old policy of isolation. The attack so far has been feeble and Rosebery is evidently not going to adopt what he sees would be an unpopular attitude.[22]

On the whole, the opposition to the abandonment of the 'old policy of isolation' was limited in extent and was neither bitter nor prolonged.

In various capitals diplomats assiduously penned dispatches reproducing the general verdict.[23] From Berlin de Noailles, the French ambassador, commented on the German reaction to Japan's achievement in having caused Britain to emerge from her 'splendid isolation', in which, he added, 'elle se complaisait orgeuilleusement et dont elle semblait vouloir faire un principe intangible de sa politique'.[24] Even those who, like Paul Cambon in London, understandably avoided what was now a hackneyed phrase, agreed that Britain had abandoned a long-established principle of her foreign policy.[25]

Epilogue

HOWEVER many differences of opinion there may previously have been as to whether Britain was really 'isolated', what precisely this 'isolation' meant, whether her alleged 'isolation' was or was not a policy, and whether it was or was not 'splendid', these differences vanished in February 1902. Britain's 'isolation', in all its assorted connotations, had come to an end with the signature of the alliance with Japan. On this point there was general agreement among those who still favoured such terminology.

To the historian it may well seem that, in so far as Britain ever had a policy of 'isolation' at all — and one's opinion concerning that point must clearly depend on how one defines the relevant term — that policy continued for several years after February 1902, at least as far as Europe was concerned. In January 1906 a new Liberal Foreign Secretary, Sir Edward Grey, still upheld, not, indeed, a policy of 'isolation' in so many words, but at least the view that 'alliances, especially continental alliances are not in accordance with our traditions'.[1]

To the historian, too, it may seem that, although the alliance with Japan did involve an important question of principle, concerning which a great deal was said and written in 1901 and 1902, it was, nevertheless, a step, whose consequences were less grave than those of other undertakings given specifically or by implication by Britain in the years that followed. By her joint declaration with France, signed by Lansdowne on 8 April 1904, Britain publicly promised to give France diplomatic support in carrying out the provisions of the declaration that related to Morocco; secretly she also anticipated the collapse of the authority of the legitimate government of that country and its division into spheres of influence. On 15 January 1906 Grey authorized conversations between the War Office and the French military authorities. Six years later new British and French naval dispositions meant that the north coast of France would, in the event of war with Germany, be exposed to attack from the sea, unless Britain were to take steps to prevent it. In the history of Britain's involvement in the rivalries of the great powers which culminated in the conflagration of 1914 these decisions naturally appear as of greater significance than the 'new departure' of 30 January 1902.

This book is, however, a study of the ideas, not of historians, but of people who lived in the years during which Britain's 'splendid isolation' was a matter of general, even if often imperfectly informed or ironical, comment. The fact is that after February 1902 little was heard, at least in connexion with Britain's foreign relations, of what Rosebery six years previously had called the 'policy of isolation, splendid or otherwise',[2] except by way of retrospect and, occasionally, of nostalgia.

A Note on Sources

MANY of the ideas concerning Britain's international position and the principles of her foreign policy were expressed in public and more particularly in Parliament. The most valuable source for their study is, accordingly, Hansard's *Parliamentary Debates*. Since 'splendid isolation' is a phrase of Canadian origin and its meaning was discussed more fully in Canada than in Britain, the *Debates of the House of Commons of the Dominion of Canada* are also an indispensable source. All the principal public speeches of the leading British politicians of the period were printed in full in *The Times*, and, unless otherwise stated, all quotations from speeches delivered outside Parliament are taken from that journal. *The Times*'s reports of debates in Parliament are occasionally fuller and apparently more accurate than those printed in Hansard's *Parliamentary Debates*, and, where this is the case, I have cited the version in *The Times*.

I have, needless to say, used the Foreign Office papers, preserved at the Public Record Office, up to the point, at least, at which the operation of the law of diminishing returns began to make itself felt. So far as reports of comments on Britain's alleged 'isolation' are concerned the most illuminating documents in this archive are the reports of Sir Edward Malet and of Colonel (later General) Leopold Swaine, who were, respectively, ambassador and military attaché in Berlin. There is, however, comparatively little to be found in the Foreign

Office papers concerning 'splendid isolation', which was a term more popular with politicians and journalists than with professional diplomats. The Foreign Office papers are, too, only moderately rich in enunciations of principles of foreign policy, and, in any case, a number of dispatches in which such principles were enunciated have been printed in Harold Temperley and Lillian M. Penson's valuable *Foundations of British Foreign Policy* (Cambridge, 1938).

I have also done my best to consult the private papers of all those who played a part of any importance in the making of British foreign policy in the years under review. In this connexion the Royal Archives at Windsor Castle are of outstanding importance. The Salisbury Papers at Christ Church, Oxford, are of great value, and the Disraeli Papers in the Hughenden Archives, the Rosebery Papers in the National Library of Scotland and the Balfour Papers at the British Museum are all of interest, as are the papers of various statesmen and ambassadors at the Public Records Office. References to those collections of papers that have yielded matter of importance will be found in the notes, together with, where necessary, an indication of their whereabouts. Several collections of private papers that I consulted proved, however, to contain nothing of significance from the point of view of the subject of this book. Some other collections, which I would have liked to be able to consult, were unfortunately not accessible.

The most convenient source for the texts of Britain's treaties and conventions during the greater part of the nineteenth century is the four-volume work by Edward Hertslet, *The Map of Europe by Treaty* (London, 1875–91), which, however, gives only the English texts. The French texts are to be found in the multi-volume *British*

and Foreign State Papers (in progress). The texts of some
of the chief agreements to which Britain was a party in the
period 1887–1902 are printed in *British Documents on the
Origins of the War, 1898–1914*, edited by G. P. Gooch
and Harold Temperley (London, 1927–38).

The 'blue-books' of 1859, 1871 and 1899, which
contain the texts of all treaties and conventions that
entailed the *casus belli* and were recognized as binding at
the times concerned, are an important source for the study
of official opinion concerning Britain's treaty obligations.
The page-references to these 'blue-books' given here
relate to the bound volumes of *Accounts and Papers* in the
State Paper Room at the British Museum. Information
concerning the dates on which they were laid before
Parliament can be found in Harold Temperley and Lillian
M. Penson's *A Century of Diplomatic Blue-Books* (London,
1966). Their genesis and significance are discussed in the
late Dame Lillian Penson's article, 'Obligations by
Treaty: Their Place in British Foreign Policy, 1898–
1914', in *Studies in Diplomatic History and Historiography in
honour of G. P. Gooch, C.H.*, edited by A. O. Sarkissian
(London, 1961), my use of which I should like to
acknowledge. Another important source for a study of
official opinion is the War Office's 'Memorandum on our
Military responsibilities with regard to Belgium, Holland,
Norway, Sweden and Portugal' with minutes thereon by
Salisbury, Lansdowne and Sanderson. The manuscript of
the memorandum is among the War Office Papers at the
Public Record Office. The memorandum and the
accompanying minutes have been printed under the title
of 'Great Britain's European Treaty Obligations in
March 1902' by Valerie Cromwell in the *Historical
Journal*, vi (1963), pp. 272–9.

The daily press of Britain, Canada and of continental countries, especially Germany, is also an important source. The files of the leading weeklies, such as the *Saturday Review* and the *Spectator*, and of reviews, such as the *Contemporary*, the *Fortnightly*, the *Nineteenth Century* and the *Quarterly* are also of interest. It is not suggested that the press influenced government policy in the period under review, but it certainly influenced the way in which many people, including prominent politicians, expressed themselves on the subject of foreign policy. The British Museum Newspaper Library at Colindale contains an invaluable collection of files of the daily and weekly press, including many foreign newspapers. An indispensable guide to this material is Oron James Hale's *Publicity and Diplomacy with special reference to England and Germany, 1890–1914* (New York, 1940).

On the other hand, the number of books on foreign policy published in Britain during the period covered by this study is not large, a fact which is itself of some significance. By far the most interesting are *The Present Position of European Politics* (London, 1887) by 'The Author of *Greater Britain*' (Sir Charles Dilke) and H. Spenser Wilkinson's *The Nation's Awakening* (London, 1896). Wilkinson's book was published at the very period at which Britain's 'isolation' was being so much discussed in the press, on the platform and in the House of Commons. Wilkinson was the brother-in-law of Eyre Crowe of the Foreign Office.

Notes

ABBREVIATIONS

(Other than those in common use)

A.P.   *Accounts and Papers.*

B.D.   *British Documents on the Origins of the War, 1898–1914,* ed. G. P. Gooch and Harold Temperley.

Debates   *Debates of the House of Commons of the Dominion of Canada.*

D.D.F. 1, 2 and 3   *Documents diplomatiques français, 1871–1914,* 1re, 2e et 3e séries.

Foundations   *Foundations of British Foreign Policy,* ed. Harold Temperley and Lillian M. Penson (Cambridge, 1938).

G.P.   *Die grosse Politik der europäischen Kabinette, 1871–1914,* ed. Johannes Leipsius, Albrecht Mendelssohn Bartholdy and Friedrich Thimme.

G.P.F.H.   *Die geheimen Papiere Friedrich von Holsteins,* ed. Norman Rich and M. H. Fisher, 4 vols. (Göttingen, 1955–63).

Hansard, 1, 2, 3 and 4   Hansard's *Parliamentary Debates,* 1st, 2nd, 3rd and 4th series.

H.J.   *Historical Journal.*

H.P.   Hughenden Papers.

J.M.H.   *Journal of Modern History.*

L.Q.V., 1, 2 and 3   *The Letters of Queen Victoria,* ed. A. C. Benson, Viscount Esher and G. E. Buckle, 1st, 2nd and 3rd series.

R.A.   Royal Archives.

R.P.   Rosebery Papers.

S.P.   Salisbury Papers.

INTRODUCTION

1. *B.D.*, ii, p. 7.
2. A. F. Pribram, *England and the International Policy of the European Great Powers, 1871–1914* (Oxford, 1931), p. 92.
3. F. Gosses, *The Management of British Foreign Policy before the First World War* (Leyden, 1948), p. 98.
4. Pribram, op. cit., p. 58; Gosses, op. cit., p. 98.
5. p. 353.
6. p. 261.
7. Lillian M. Penson, 'Obligations by Treaty: Their Place in British Foreign Policy, 1898–1914', in *Studies in Diplomatic History and Historiography in honour of G. P. Gooch, C.H.*, ed. A. O. Sarkissian (London, 1961), pp. 76, 88.
8. A. J. P. Taylor, *The Struggle for Mastery in Europe* (Oxford, 1954), p. 400.
9. See above, notes 1–3.
10. Hajo Holborn, *Der Zusammenbruch des europäischen Staatensystems* (Stuttgart, 1955), p. 51.
11. Hans Herzfeld, *Die moderne Welt, 1789–1945* (Brunswick, 1960), ii, p. 38.
12. Taylor, op. cit., p. 352.
13. Lady Gwendolen Cecil, *Life of Robert, Marquis of Salisbury*, 5 vols. (London, 1921–32), iv, p. 85.
14. E.g., R. C. K. Ensor, *England, 1870–1914* (Oxford, 1936), p. 350. Many other examples could be cited.
15. Taylor, op. cit., p. 400.
16. *J.M.H.*, xxxi (1959), p. 27.
17. *H.J.*, vii (1964), p. 342.

CHAPTER ONE: BRITAIN'S CONSCIOUSNESS OF 'ISOLATION'

1. James Boswell, *Life of Johnson*, 21 March 1783, quoted *O.E.D.*
2. *Later Correspondence of Lord John Russell, 1840–1878*, ed. G. P. Gooch (London, 1925), ii, p. 99.
3. *Hansard*, 3, clxxvi, col. 1023, 7 July 1864.
4. *Hansard*, 3, ccxciv, col. 853, 19 Feb. 1885.

5. See Theodor A. Bayer, *England und der neue Kurs, 1890–1895* (Tübingen, 1955), pp. 80–95.

6. Oron James Hale, *Publicity and Diplomacy, 1890–1914* (New York, 1940), pp. 87–101.

7. *The Times*, 10 Nov. 1894.

8. Malet to Kimberley, 14 Dec. 1894, F.O. 64/1326.

9. *Hamburgischer Correspondent*, 11 Nov. 1894.

10. *Standard*, 12 Nov. 1894.

11. Hale, op. cit., pp. 26–7.

12. On 13 March 1887 Salisbury wrote to Queen Victoria to return some papers, apropos of which he observed: 'The only unsatisfactory part is that which shows that the Sultan takes his views of English policy from the columns of the Standard. We have no influence with the paper by which we could keep it from any line of writing or tone of policy that we disapproved. Occasionally it will put in what it is asked to put in: but this is very rare. The paper is quite independent: but we have to bear the blame of its proceedings.' (R.A. A. 65/61.)

13. *Standard*, 16 Nov. 1894.

14. *Hamburgischer Correspondent*, 18 Nov. 1894.

15. Hale, op. cit., p. 48.

16. *Kölnische Zeitung*, 20 Nov. 1894.

17. *Standard*, 19 and 21 Nov. 1894, reporting comments in other German newspapers.

18. Malet to Kimberley, 8 Dec. 1894, F.O. 64/1326.

19. Malet to Salisbury, 7 July 1895, Bayer, op. cit., p. 124.

20. Swaine, memorandum, 15 Nov. 1894 (copy), R.A. H. 46/86.

21. Malet to Kimberley, 16 Jan. 1895, F.O. 64/1350.

22. Queen Victoria to Kimberley, 27 April 1895 (copy), R.A. Q. 16/94.

23. *The Times*, 11 June 1895.

24. *Standard*, 5 Aug. 1895.

25. Drummond to Salisbury, 24 Aug. 1895, F.O. 9/270.

26. Hale, op. cit., p. 106.

27. William II to Queen Victoria, 8 Jan. 1896 (copy), R.A. O. 45/140a.

28. J. A. S. Grenville, *Lord Salisbury and Foreign Policy* (London, 1964), p. 39.

29. Grenville, op. cit., pp. 40–42.

30. *G.P.* xi, p. 10. (English and French in the original.)

31. *The Times* and other newspapers, 19 and 20 Dec. 1895.

32. Swaine, memorandum, 20 Dec. 1895, F.O. 64/1351.

33. *The Times* and other newspapers, 9 and 10 Jan. 1896.

34. Deym to Goluchowski, 23 Jan. 1896, printed by E. Walters, *Slavonic Review*, xxix (1950–1), p. 277.

35. Malet to Rosebery, 22 Dec. 1894, R.P. Box 91.

36. *G.P.*, xi, pp. 68, 71; *G.P.F.H.*, iii, p. 520; Lascelles to Salisbury, 21 Dec. 1895, F.O. 64/1351.

37. *L.Q.V.*, 3, iii, p. 21.

38. *L.Q.V.*, 3, iii, p. 22.

39. *Punch*, 18 Jan. 1896.

40. Add. MS. 48668.

41. Mary Gladstone, *Diaries and Letters*, ed. Lucy Masterman (London, 1930), p. 430.

42. Wilfrid Scawen Blunt, *My Diaries* (London, 1932), p. 212.

43. *National Review*, xxviii (1896), p. 227.

44. *Hansard*, 4, xxxvi, col. 3, 11 Feb. 1896.

45. Herbert Bismarck to Rosebery, 17 Feb. 1896, R.P. Box 5; Chirol, memorandum, 25 Jan. 1896, S.P. A. 120/27.

46. Malet to Rosebery, 22 Dec. 1894, R.P. Box 91.

47. Rosebery to Ripon, 5 Jan. 1896, Add. MS. 43516.

48. William II to Queen Victoria, 8 Jan. 1896 (copy), R.A. O/140a.

49. Lascelles to Salisbury, 7 March 1896, S.P. A 122/29.

50. Dufferin and Ava to Queen Victoria, 1 Jan. 1896, R.A. J. 90/21.

51. Monson to Salisbury, 12 Jan. 1896, F.O. 7/1241.

52. C. F. G. Stanley, *Canada's Soldiers* (Toronto, 1954), p. 274.

53. *The Times*, 13 Jan. 1896.

54. Grenville, op. cit., p. 68.

55. Salisbury to Queen Victoria, 11 Jan. 1896, R.A. A. 72/45.

56. *Standard*, 9 Jan. 1896.

57. *Morning Post*, 22 Jan. 1896.

58. *G.P.*, xi, p. 53.

59. Kimberley to Rosebery, 14 Nov. 1896, R.P. Box 54.

60. Rosebery to Kimberley, 28 Nov. 1896 (copy), R.P. Box 54.

61. Kimberley to Rosebery, 14 Nov. 1896, R.P. Box 54.

CHAPTER TWO: 'SPLENDID BUT DANGEROUS ISOLATION'

1. *Debates*, xli, col. 176, 16 Jan. 1896.
2. *Debates*, xli, col. 189, 16 Jan. 1896.
3. *The Times*, 18 Jan. 1896.
4. *The Times*, 22 Jan. 1896.
5. *Spectator*, 25 Jan. 1896; *Sunday Times*, 26 Jan. 1896.
6. Stanley, op. cit., p. 274.
7. *Debates*, xli, col. 4, 2 Jan. 1896.
8. Reported in *Globe* (Toronto), 12 Jan. 1896.
9. *Globe*, 9 Jan. 1896.
10. *Globe*, 15 Jan. 1896.
11. *The Times*, 18 Jan. 1896.
12. *Debates*, xli, cols. 1186–1222, 5 Feb. 1896.
13. *Debates*, xli, col. 1197, 5 Feb. 1896.
14. *Globe*, 17 Jan. 1896.
15. W. S. Gilbert, *Utopia Limited* (London, 1893), Act I, p. 4.
16. *Debates*, xli, col. 176, 16 Jan. 1896.
17. *Debates*, xli, col. 1215, 5 Feb. 1896.
18. *Debates*, xli, col. 176, 16 Jan. 1896.
19. *Debates*, xli, col. 1191, 5 Feb. 1896.
20. *Debates*, xli, col. 1216, 5 Feb. 1896.
21. *The Times*, 22 Jan. 1896.
22. *Spectator*, 25 Jan. 1896.
23. *The Times*, 7 Jan. 1902.
24. *G.P.*, xvii, pp. 19, 97; *G.P.F.H.*, iv, p. 74.
25. *Nineteenth Century*, xl (1896), p. 684.

CHAPTER THREE: 'ISOLATION' AS A POLICY

1. *Hansard*, 3, clxxiii, col. 81, 4 Feb. 1864; clxxxvii, col. 1910, 14 June 1867.
2. *Hansard*, 3, cciv, col. 397, 17 Feb. 1871.
3. Cecil, op. cit., ii, p. 132.
4. *Contemporary Review*, lxvii (1895), p. 838; lxviii (1895), p. 629; lxix (1896), p. 166; *Speaker*, 18 Jan. 1896; *Spectator*, 25 Jan. 1896; *Saturday Review*, 25 Jan. 1896.
5. *The Times*, 27 Feb. 1896.

6. *The Times*, 4 March 1896.

7. *The Times*, 4 March 1896.

8. *Hansard*, 4, xxxviii, col. 248, 5 March 1896.

9. *Hansard*, 4, xxxviii, col. 269, 5 March 1896.

10. H. Spenser Wilkinson, *The Nation's Awakening* (London, 1896), p. 143.

11. E.g., the reports in *Hansard* of the Commons debates of 5 March 1896, 5 April and 10 June 1898, and 13 Feb. 1902, and of the Lords debate of 13 Feb. 1902.

12. *Hansard*, 3, cccxiii, col. 38, 31 March 1887.

13. Dufferin and Ava to Queen Victoria, 13 Oct. 1895, R.A. J. 90/18.

14. *Hansard*, 4, cii, col. 1293, 13 Feb. 1902.

CHAPTER FOUR: 'JARGON ABOUT ISOLATION'

1. It is not the purpose of this chapter to re-tell in detail the story of the 'scramble for China' or of the attempts made in the years 1898–1901 to bring about an Anglo-German alliance, concerning both of which subjects there is already an abundant literature. See J. L. Garvin, *Life of Joseph Chamberlain*, iii (London, 1934); Julian Amery, *Life of Joseph Chamberlain*, iv (London, 1951); A. Malozemoff, *Russian Far Eastern Policy, 1881–1904* (Berkeley, 1958); George Monger, *The End of Isolation* (London, 1963); Grenville, op. cit. My aim is simply to trace the course of the controversy over Britain's alleged policy of 'isolation'.

2. Garvin, op. cit., iii, pp. 259–60.

3. Garvin, op. cit., iii, pp. 263–77.

4. *Hansard*, 4, lvi, col. 281, 5 April 1898.

5. *The Times*, 6 April 1898, which gives a fuller report than that in *Hansard*.

6. *The Times*, 5 May 1898.

7. *The Times*, 14 May 1898.

8. *Hansard*, 4, lviii, cols. 1338, 1347, 1419, 10 June 1898.

9. *St James's Gazette, Standard, Telegraph* and *The Times*, 14 May 1898.

10. *Hansard*, 4, lvii, col. 1513, 17 May 1898.

11. *Hansard*, 4, lvii, col. 1515, 17 May 1898.

12. *Hansard*, 4, lviii, col. 1338, 10 June 1898.
13. *Hansard*, 4, lviii, col. 1350.
14. *Hansard*, 4, lviii, cols. 1375, 1418.
15. *Hansard*, 4, lviii, col. 1432.
16. Garvin, op. cit., iii, p. 279.
17. Lascelles to Salisbury, 27 May 1898, S.P. A. 121/10.
18. *The Times*, 9 Dec. 1898.
19. *G.P.*, xv, pp. 413–18.
20. Garvin, op. cit., iii, p. 506.
21. *The Times*, 1 Dec. 1899.
22. *The Times* and *Daily News*, 1 Dec. 1899; Hale, op. cit., pp. 212–14.
23. Chamberlain to Lascelles, 12 Dec. 1899, Lascelles Papers, F.O. 800/9.
24. Hermann, Freiherr von Eckardstein, *Lebenserinnerungen und politische Denkwürdigkeiten* (Leipzig, 1920), ii, p. 236.
25. *B.D.*, ii, p. 60.
26. *B.D.*, ii, p. 65.
27. *B.D.*, ii, p. 68.
28. *B.D.*, ii, pp. 73–6.
29. Monger, op. cit., p. 65.

CHAPTER FIVE: THE 'TRADITIONAL POLICY'

1. *Hansard*, 3, clxxxiv, col. 736, 9 July 1866.
2. *The Times*, 4 March 1896.
3. *Foundations, passim*.
4. *Hansard*, 4, lviii, col. 1338, 10 June 1898; *B.D.*, i, p. 162.
5. Salisbury to Lascelles, 10 March 1896, Lascelles Papers, F.O. 800/9.
6. *The Times*, 14 April 1897; *Hansard*, 4, lviii, col. 1420, 10 June 1898.
7. *Hansard*, 4, lvii, col. 1512, 17 May 1898.
8. *Hansard*, 4, lviii, col. 1350, 10 June 1898.
9. *B.D.*, ii, p. 73.
10. *Hansard*, 4, lvii, col. 1512, 17 May 1898.
11. *Hansard*, 4, lviii, col. 1347, 10 June 1898.
12. *Hansard*, 4, cii, col. 1303, 13 Feb. 1902.

13. *Hansard*, 4, cii, col. 1276, 13 Feb. 1902.
14. *The Times*, 14 April 1897.
15. *Foundations*, p. 356.
16. See Ch. 9.
17. A. D. Elliott, *Life of Viscount Goschen* (London, 1911), ii, p. 197.
18. *Hansard*, 3, cccx, col. 63, 27 Jan. 1887.
19. *St James's Gazette*, 11 Feb. 1888; *Saturday Review*, 25 Jan., 29 Feb., 1896; see also Conservative press generally, 14 May 1898; *Contemporary Review*, lxix (1896), p. 153; Wilkinson, op. cit., p. 142.
20. *The Times*, 23 March 1880.
21. *The Present Position of European Politics* (London, 1887), by 'The Author of *Greater Britain*' (Charles W. Dilke), p. 46.
22. *Globe* (Toronto), 16 Jan. 1896.
23. Eckardstein, op. cit., ii, pp. 235–7.
24. See Ch. 10.

CHAPTER SIX: LEGEND OR REALITY?

1. Penson, op. cit., p. 88.
2. Salisbury to Queen Victoria, 5 Feb. 1887, R.A. H. 34/35.
3 *The Times*, 4 March 1896.
4. *The Times*, 14 May 1898.
5. Rosebery to Kimberley, 28 April 1895 (copy), R.P. Box 54.
6. *L.Q.V.*, 3, i, p. 272.
7. *B.D.*, viii, p. 4.
8. On 28 June 1893 Deym reported to Kálnoky, the Austro-Hungarian Foreign Minister, after a conversation the previous day with Rosebery: 'Lord Rosebery erwiderte darauf, "Ich muss Ihnen ganz aufrichtig vor Allem erklären, dass ich von dem Schriftwechsel und den Punktationen auf welche Sie sich beziehen, obwohl ihre Existenz mir bekannt ist, niemals Kenntnis genommen habe, und zwar aus dem Grunde, weil ich, wenn eine diesbezügliche Interpellation an mich gerichtet würde, in der Lage sein wollte, mit gutem Gewissen antworten zu können, dass mir dieser Schriftwechsel nicht bekannt sei." ' (Vienna Staatsarchiv, P.A. I/462.) I am indebted to Dr F. R. Bridge for this transcription. A translation of Deym's dispatch is printed in *Foundations*, p. 475.

I

9. *D.D.F.*, 1, x, p. 106.
10. Salisbury to Monson, 4 Feb. 1896, F.O. 120/721; see also J. A. S. Grenville, *Slavonic Review*, xxxvi (1957–8), p. 358, n. 49.
11. Salisbury to Lascelles, 10 March 1896, Lascelles Papers, F.O. 800/9.
12. *B.D.*, i, p. 73.
13. *B.D.*, ii, pp. 15–16.
14. For the meaning of this term see James Headlam-Morley, *Studies in Diplomatic History* (London, 1930), pp. 105–25.
15. M. R. D. Foot, 'Great Britain and Luxemburg 1867', *English Historical Review*, lxvii (1952), p. 372.
16. *Hansard*, 3, clxxxvii, col. 379, 13 May 1867.
17. *Hansard*, 3, clxxxvii, col. 1922, 14 June 1867; *Foundations*, p. 313.
18. *Hansard*, 3, cciv, col. 1373, 6 March 1871.
19. *Hansard*, 3, cxlii, col. 127, 6 May 1856.
20. *Political Correspondence of Mr Gladstone and Lord Granville, 1868–1876*, ed. Agatha Ramm (London, 1952), i, p. 182.
21. W. E. Mosse, *The Rise and Fall of the Crimean System* (London, 1963), pp. 185–201.
22. *Hansard*, 3, ccxxxii, col. 41, 8 Feb. 1877.
23. Salisbury to Soveral, 8 Oct. 1899 (copy), S.P. A. 128/109.
24. Quoted as in *B.D.*, i, 93–94.
25. *B.D.*, i, p. 50.
26. *Hansard*, 3, cccxxii, cols. 152, 377, 557, 1172–95.
27. Wilkinson, op. cit., p. 80.
28. Garvin, op. cit., iii, pp. 273–4.
29. *Pall Mall Gazette*, 3 Sept. 1898.
30. Hale, op. cit., p. 176.
31. Sanderson to Hardinge, 6 April 1904, R.A. W. 43/74.

CHAPTER SEVEN: 'A PIECE OF PAPER'

1. Penson, op. cit., p. 88.
2. *The Times*, 27 Feb. 1896.
3. *Hansard*, 3, clxxxvii, col. 1923, 14 June 1867.
4. Clarendon to Gladstone, 3 and 14 April 1869, Add. MS. 44133 see; also *L.Q.V.*, 2, ii, pp. 589–91.

5. *Hansard*, 3, cciii, col. 1787, 10 Aug. 1870.

6. Granville to Queen Victoria, 2 March 1871, R.A. B. 26/11.

7. *Hansard*, 3, cciv, cols. 1360–8, 6 March 1871.

8. A. G. Stapleton, *Political Life of George Canning* (London, 1831), i, pp. 427–30.

9. *A.P.*, Session 2 of 1859, xxxii, p. 593.

10. *Hansard*, 3, clii, col. 42, 3 Feb. 1859.

11. *Hansard*, 3, cciv, col. 1373, 6 March 1871.

12. *A.P.*, Session of 1871, lxxii (275), p. 449; (275–1), p. 555.

13. *Hansard*, 3, ccx, col. 1151, 12 April 1872.

14. *Hansard*, 3, ccx, col. 1180, 12 April 1872.

15. *The Times*, 13 April 1872, which gives a fuller report than that in *Hansard*.

16. *Hansard*, 3, ccx, col. 1178, 12 April 1872.

17. *Hansard*, 3, ccxxxii, col. 476, 16 Feb. 1877.

18. *Hansard*, 3, ccxl, col. 1409, 13 June 1878.

19. *Foundations*, pp. 156–7.

20. *Hansard*, 3, clxxxvii, col. 1923, 14 June 1867.

21. *Hansard*, 4, lxi, col. 1195, 15 July 1898.

22. *A.P.*, Session of 1899, cix (c. 9088), p. 1.

23. *Hansard*, 3, ccxlii, col. 509, 29 July 1878.

24. *D.D.F.*, 2, vi, p. 551.

25. *Hansard*, 4, xxxix, col. 449, 30 March 1896.

26. Penson, op. cit., p. 80.

27. Granville to Howden, 7 Feb. 1852 (copy), Granville Papers, G.D. 29/20. (P.R.O.)

28. *B.D.*, i, p. 51.

29. *B.D.*, ii, p. 52.

30. Lytton to Derby, 24 Dec. 1875, F.O. 63/1024; Derby to Lytton, 14 Jan. 1876, F.O. 63/1033. For a fuller discussion of the Foreign Office's attitude in the eighteen-seventies see *Foundations*, pp. 342, 512–14.

31. Salisbury to Queen Victoria, 19 Feb. 1891, R.A. J. 66/84.

32. *B.D.*, i, p. 50.

33. *A.P.*, Session of 1899, cix (c. 9088), p. 79.

34. See Ch. 6.

35. Printed, together with accompanying letters and minutes, by Valerie Cromwell, *H.J.*, vi (1963), pp. 272–9. There is an account of

this episode in Sir William Robertson's *Soldiers and Statesmen* (London, 1926), i, p. 44.

36. *H.J.*, vi (1963), p. 279.

37. Salisbury to Queen Victoria, 19 Feb. 1891, R.A. J. 66/84. See also above, n. 31.

38. Bertie to Bigge, 28 Nov. 1899, R.A. I. 62/71.

39. *H.J.*, vi, pp. 277–8.

40. See Salisbury's speech in the House of Lords, 29 July 1878, quoted in Ch. 9.

41. *Hansard*, 3, cciii, col. 1787, 10 Aug. 1870.

42. *Hansard*, 3, ccx, col. 1179, 12 April 1872.

43. *Fortnightly Review*, xli (1887), pp. 24–27, reprinted in Dilke, op. cit., pp. 42–47.

44. Dilke, op. cit., p. 44.

45. *Nouvelle Revue*, xliv (1887), p. 76.

46. Vivian to Iddesleigh, 7 Jan. 1887, F.O. 10/498.

47. Vivian to Salisbury, 18, 28 and 31 Jan. 1887, F.O. 10/498.

48. Vivian to Salisbury, 1 Feb. 1887, S.P. A. 49/1.

49. *Standard*, 4 Feb. 1887. See also Cecil, op. cit., iv, pp. 55–62.

50. *Pall Mall Gazette*, 4 Feb. 1887; *Morning Post*, 5 Feb. 1887; *National Review*, viii (1887), p. 856.

51. Vivian to Salisbury, 5 Feb. 1887, F.O. 10/498.

52. Vivian to Salisbury, 12 Feb. 1887, F.O. 10/498.

53. Cecil, op. cit., iv, p. 61.

54. Salisbury to Vivian, 11 Feb. 1887, F.O. 10/497.

55. Vivian to Salisbury, 26 Feb. 1887, F.O. 10/498.

56. For differing views on this point see, for example: Gladstone's speech in the Commons on 10 Aug. 1870 (*Hansard*, 3, cciii, col. 1786); Dilke, op. cit., pp. 46, 285; Cecil, op. cit., ii, p. 368, iii, p. 259; *H.J.*, vi (1963), p. 276.

57. *H.J.*, vi (1963), vi, pp. 275–9.

58. *The Times*, 30 July 1891.

59. *H.J.*, vi (1963), p. 279.

CHAPTER EIGHT: SALISBURY AND 'SPLENDID ISOLATION'

1. Maurice Baumont, *L'essor industriel et l'impérialisme colonial* (Paris, 1949), p. 213.

2. See Introduction.
3. *G.P.F.H.*, iii, p. 535. (English in original.)
4. *B.D.*, ii, p. 85.
5. Balfour, memorandum, 12 Dec. 1902, Add. MS. 49727.
6. *Saturday Review*, 25 Jan. 1896.
7. *Cambridge History of British Foreign Policy* (Cambridge, 1923), iii, p. 261.
8. Cecil, op. cit., iv, p. 85.
9. *Quarterly Review*, cxi (1862), p. 235.
10. *Hansard*, 3, ccxciv, col. 853, 19 Feb. 1885: Cecil, op. cit. iii, p. 226.
11. Cecil, op. cit., ii, p. 132.
12. Salisbury to Queen Victoria, 5 Feb. 1887, R.A. H. 34/35; speech at Caernarvon, 10 April 1888, quoted on p. 73.
13. *L.Q.V.*, 3, i, p. 272.
14. *L.Q.V.*, 3, i, p. 437.
15. *L.Q.V.*, 3, iii, p. 21.
16. *The Times*, 5 May 1898. (See Ch. 4.)
17. *B.D.*, ii, p. 68.
18. *The Times*, 10 Nov. 1896.
19. *Hansard*, 4, lxxviii, col. 31, 30 Jan. 1900.
20. *The Times*, 11 April 1888.
21. *Quarterly Review*, cxcvi (1902), p. 664.
22. Blunt, op. cit., p. 483.
23. Lord Rosebery, *Miscellanies* (London, 1921), i, pp. 264–74.
24. Victoria Hicks Beach, *Life of Sir Michael Hicks Beach* (London, 1916), ii, pp. 359–63.

CHAPTER NINE: SALISBURY AND THE *casus belli*

1. *Foundations*, p. 313.
2. Otto von Bismarck, *Gedanken und Erinnerungen* (Stuttgart, 1898), ii, p. 235; *G.P.*, xiv, p. 199; *B.D.*, i, p. 249. There are many other examples.
3. Arnold Heeren, *Historische Werke* (Göttingen, 1821), i, p. 272.
4. Cecil, op. cit., iv, p. 404.
5. Salisbury to Monson, 4 Feb. 1896, F.O. 120/721.
6. *Foundations*, p. 497.

7. *Hansard*, 3, cccxliv, col. 1062, 16 May 1890.
8. *B.D.*, ii, p. 68.
9. *L.Q.V.*, 3, iii, p. 21; *B.D.*, ii, p. 69.
10. Cecil, op. cit., ii, pp. 127, 365–9.
11. Salisbury to Beaconsfield, 12 Oct. 1879. H.P. Box 93.
12. Northcote to Beaconsfield, 30 Oct. 1879. H.P. Box 107.
13. *Hansard*, 3, ccxlii, col. 509, 29 July 1878.
14. *L.Q.V.*, 3, i, p. 268.
15. Salisbury, memorandum, 23 Feb. 1887, R.A. H. 34/42.
16. *Hansard*, 3, ccxli, col. 1804, 18 July 1878.
17. *The Times*, 22 July 1878.
18. Salisbury to Beaconsfield, 7 April 1880, H.P. Box 93.
19. Cecil, op. cit., ii, p. 380.
20. *D.D.F.*, 1, vii, pp. 5–7.
21. *D.D.F.*, 1, vii, p. 42.
22. See Ch. 5.
23. See Ch. 7.
24. Cecil, op. cit., ii, p. 370.
25. Rosebery to Gladstone, 16 July 1891, Add. MS. 44289.
26. A. G. Gardiner, *Life of Sir William Harcourt* (London, 1923), ii, p. 153.
27. *D.D.F.*, 1, ix, p. 225.
28. Gardiner, op. cit., ii, p. 449.
29. Algernon West, *Private Diaries* (London, 1923), p. 295.
30. *Daily News*, 1 Dec. 1899.
31. *B.D.*, ii, p. 108.

CHAPTER TEN: 'RECANTATION'

1. Ian H. Nish, *The Anglo-Japanese Alliance* (London, 1966).
2. Quoted at length by Zara S. Steiner, *J.M.H.*, xxxi (1959), p. 30.
3. Nish, op. cit., p. 175.
4. Presumably a slip for 'July'.
5. Salisbury to King Edward VII, 5 Nov. 1902, R.A. R. 22/57.
6. Balfour, memorandum. 12 Dec. 1901, Add. MS. 49727.
7. Ibid.
8. Cab. 37/60. No. 1. (P.R.O.)

9. Memorandum, 7 Jan. 1902, S.P. Cabinet Papers, Box 5; Cab. 37/60. No. 3. (P.R.O.)
10. *B. D.*, ii, pp. 114–20.
11. Hicks Beach, op. cit., ii, p. 362.
12. Add. MS. 48679.
13. *Spectator*, 15 Feb. 1902.
14. *Daily News*, 13 Feb. 1902.
15. *Daily Chronicle*, 12 Feb. 1902.
16. *The Times*, 13 Feb. 1902.
17. *Hansard*, 4, cii, cols. 1173, 1273, 1293, 1301, 13 Feb. 1902.
18. *Hansard*, 4, cii, col. 1303.
19. *Hansard*, 4, cii, col. 1311.
20. *Hansard*, 4, cii, cols. 1175–6.
21. *The Times*, 15 Feb. 1902.
22. Lansdowne to Curzon, 16 Feb. 1902, Curzon Papers, MSS. Eur. F. 11, vol. 151. (India Office Library.)
23. Lascelles to Lansdowne, 14 Feb. 1902, F.O. 64/1551; *G.P.*, xvii, p. 152.
24. *D. D.F.*, 2, ii, p. 106.
25. *D. D.F.*, 2, ii, p. 101.

EPILOGUE

1. *B. D.*, iii, p. 177.
2. *The Times*, 4 March 1896.

Index

DATE DUE

MY 4 '77			
AP 8 '83			
FEB 3 '86			
FEB 11 '86			
FEB 24 '86			
MAR 28 '86			
MAR 28 '86			
			PRINTED IN U.S.A.
GAYLORD			